GLOW OF SILENT TRUTHS

By
Rajeev K. Moudgil

Copyright ©Rajeev K. Moudgil, 2025

All rights reserved.

No part of this publication may be reproduced, transmitted or stored in a retrieval system, in any form or by any means, electronic, mechanical, photocopying, recording or otherwise, without the prior permission of the publisher, except in the case of brief quotations embodied in critical articles or reviews permitted by copyright law.

Disclaimer: No liability is assumed for errors or omissions.

Paperback ISBN 978 9 334 24353 6
eBook ISBN   978 9 334 24744 2

First Edition.

Published by: Rajeev K. Moudgil
1875, Sector-23, Gurugram-122017, India.

Printed by: IngramSpark

Dedicated to
the memory of
my parents

To
my wife Ritu
and daughters
Divya and Suchitra

Foreword

Glow of Silent Truths presents a collection of my observations and reflections on the experiences of life. In it every piece starts with a new theme, and explores the silent truth, which is not readily apparent in the normal thinking and sometimes counter-intuitive.

The silent truths of this book are transient like much else in life, but they mostly hold up in the conditions in which we live. Reflecting on both subtle and obvious truths illuminates new paths of our thinking. The very act of reflections makes the silent truths glow.

It is an endeavor to enhance the clarity of mind and to offer insights into the human behavior by bringing out the beauty of silent truths.

Many silent truths of the book will find resonance with the personal experiences of the reader.

The book has not been divided into chapters because there is no structure to the flow of thoughts, they arise and subside on their own. The book got written on its own as thoughts emerged during walks, reading, quiet moments, the chores, and even sleepless nights.

The book explores themes of existence, self, truth, emotions, knowledge, conduct, and social constructs.

There is ample scope for readers to disagree with the interpretations of the book, but reading it will surely make them think afresh about many truths of life.

If the book sparks surprise, delight or just reflections, then I will be satisfied with my efforts.

I hope readers will find as much joy in reading the book as I did in writing it.

...

CONTENTS

Blessings	1
Questions	2
Clouds	3
Living In The Hope	4
Dream of Living	5
One or Many	6
Forgetting	7
Dance of Fire	8
Naming and Knowing	9
Desire	10
Small	11
Expansion	12
Known	13
Words	14
Imitation	15
Reaction	16
Release	17
Shades of Truth	18
Timing	19
Contradiction	20
Self-assertion	21
Defensiveness	22

Discovery	23
Cry	24
Wave of Existence	25
Pain	26
The Tree	27
Past	28
Wheel of Karma	29
Nostalgia	30
Knowing	31
Opening	32
Transition	33
Feedback	34
Interaction	35
Meditation	36
Disguised Truths	37
Numbers	38
Attention	39
Control	40
Infinite	41
Seeking Bliss	42
Virtue	43
Prayer	44
Manifested World	45
Description	46

Search	47
Showing off	48
Tears	49
Interregnum	50
Curiosity	51
Aspiration	52
Rare	53
Danger	54
Obligations	55
Prediction	56
Innocence	57
Limits	58
Experience	59
Unequal world	60
God	61
Puzzle	62
Void	63
Extinction	64
Dreams	65
Happiness	66
Time	67
Passionate Strivers	68
Poise of Mind	69
Forests	70

Restlessness	71
Message	72
Trouble	73
Compulsion	74
Principles	75
Assumptions	76
Talent	77
Anarchy	78
Renunciation	79
Stranger	80
Pretense	81
Unconscious	82
Objective Reality	83
Fear	84
Expectation	85
Trust	86
Darkness	87
Sky	88
Renewal	89
Promise	90
Stress	91
Center	92
Moments	93
Schemer	94

Transient Truths	95
Reflections	96
Revenge	97
Watch	98
Cage	99
Possession	100
Secret	101
Abundance	102
Silence	103
Anger	104
Beauty	105
Envy	106
Freedom	107
Boundary	108
Imagination	109
Thinking	110
Indifference	111
Wronged	112
Attraction	113
Flow	114
Opportunity	115
Playfulness	116
Defeat	117
Inefficiency	118

Compass	119
Hate	120
Inspiration	121
Win	122
Attachment	123
Success	124
Risk	125
Light	126
Acceptance	127
Moment of Truth	128
Politics	129
Exit	130
Compromise	131
Timeless	132
False Knowledge	133
Oppression	134
Rise and Fall	135
Living in the Moment	136
Distraction	137
Choice	138
Horizon	139
Dimensions	140
Anchor	141
Walking	142

Comparison	143
Discipline	144
Art	145
Signs	146
Colors	147
Aroma	148
Identity	149
Space	150
Mountains	151
Mystery of Truth	152
Equality	153
Far and Near	154
Implicit Order	155
The Way	156
Familiarity	157
Teaching	158
Escape	159
Learning	160
Belief	161
Privacy	162
Mind	163
Logic	164
Unhurried life	165
Traveling	166

Technology	167
Betrayal	168
Paradox of Living	169
Mistakes	170
Power of Money	171
Sacred is Private	172
Self and Ego	173
Liberty	174
Focus	175
A City	176
The Fear of Freedom	177
Fooled Forever	178
Culture	179
Rocks	180
Health	181
Fire	182
Witness	183
The River	184
Pleasures	185
Night	186
Wind	187
Shadow	188
Waiting	189
Easy Life	190

Lost and Found	191
Metaphor	192
Imagine	193
Love	194
Game Theory	195
Enemy	196
Optimism	197
Affluence	198
Fullness	199
Motivation	200
Humor	201
Ambiguity	202
Fragile	203
Validation	204
Meaning	205
Power	206
Duality	207
Silent Truths	208
Beyond the Obvious	209
Failures	210
Change	211
Sleep	212
Cause and Effect	213
Wisdom	214

Memory	215
Sameness	216
Negative	217
Price of Money	218
Complexity	219
Boat	220
Kindness	221
Mirror	222
Journey	223
Nothing Matters	224
Noise	225
Temptations	226
Ignorance	227
Rain	228
Belonging	229
Diversity	230
Sacrifice	231
Morality in Art	232
Solitude	233
Letting Go	234

Blessings

A bad outcome in life
often happens to avert
a bigger disaster.

A minor illness may
prevent a life-threatening
disease later in life.

Obstacles and failures
in our life journey are
devices that protect
and assist us.

Reflections on the past
show that often failures
turn out to be blessings
in disguise.

Many blessings of life
come in the form of
failures, illnesses,
and obstacles.

...

Questions

A right question expands
the knowledge, while
right answers only repeat
what is already known.

Unknowns are solved
by the right questions;
only knowns have
ready answers.

All analyses are about
asking questions, not
for giving answers.

We search in vain
for the purpose of life
because we search answers,
not questions.

It is questioning that
leads to truth;
answers often drag us
to falsehood.

...

Glow of Silent Truths

Clouds

Clouds bring
rain and shade, and
thunder and lightning.

Some clouds block
the sunshine, while
others provide relief
in the hot summer.

For some, clouds
bring prosperity; for
others, disaster.

Myriad shapes in the
clouds inspire onlookers
and some read the future
in them.

Clouds are like our fate:
both load slowly and
splash suddenly.

...

Living In The Hope

We know not what
seeks us, yet live in the
hope of being found.

We exist in the void of
the sky and are drawn
to the light.

We sleep to wake up in
the future and love to
make a new us.

We smile in praise of
what is, and we pray
when in tears.

We chase the dreams
unseen and live in
the hope of being
found.

...

Glow of Silent Truths

Dream of Living

We live our life,
yet forget that
we are living it.

When we dream,
we truly live
that dream.

So, we are mostly
unaware while living,
and mindful while
dreaming.

Who knows if
dreaming is living,
and living is just
a dream?

…

Glow of Silent Truths

One or Many

We are one with many
and many make us one.

The one tells us there is
one outside, but the many
inside sense many outside.

Only one among the
many is real, and many
inside are unreal.

The many shape the
one outside into their
own image -- many.

The disguised truth is
that there is only one,
outside and inside.

...

Glow of Silent Truths

Forgetting

We do not remember what
we have forgotten,
forgetting leaves a void
we cannot enter.

It is strange that we know
that we forget, what we
forget is not known.

It's like dying--we know what dying is,
but don't really know what dying is.

Dying and forgetting run in parallel;
when we forget, something dies within us.

We forget the hurts we caused
to others, we forget our acts done
out of arrogance.

We forget how others helped us,
we forget how we are aided at
every step of life.

After death all that is forgotten
survives, forgotten things
remake us afterwards.

...

Glow of Silent Truths

Dance of Fire

Everything comes from
the fire we call light;
everything subsists in
the sky we call space.

Who lit the first fire and
created the first point in
the sky, and which of these
two came first?

All existence is a dance of
the light in the space;
who is directing the moves of
this dance?

Is this dance separate
from the one who is
directing it?

Perhaps the dancer is
dancing to its own tunes.

...

Naming and Knowing

If we know the name
of a thing, it no
longer bothers us.

But if we do not know the
name of the thing, there is
a kind of restlessness inside.

For us, labeling something
with a name is knowing;
not knowing the name
makes us restless.

This disquiet is not really
for not knowing the name,
but it is for not knowing at all.

We need to remind ourselves
knowing the name is not
the same as knowing.

We hope in vain that knowing
the name would somehow
enable us to know reality.

...

Glow of Silent Truths

Desire

What is it that

drives us to the sky,

makes us love,

inspires us to strive,

yearns for drink,

pulsates in the heart,

craves for lust,

prods us to do more, and

prompts us to remain hopeful.

It is the desire to be what we are not.

...

Small

Small atoms make stars,
and little drops, oceans;
vastness is a collection of
small spaces.

All growths and decays are
small successes or failures
added over time.

Diseases are caused by
small germs and treated
by small molecules.

Small strands of DNA
make who we are, and
a good life is made of
small routines.

Small things exist,
and large things are
the outcomes of small
things in harmony.

...

Glow of Silent Truths

Expansion

It is the expansion of
the space from which
emerged many worlds.

As a result, expansion is
a companion to growth
in many aspects of existence.

Expansion of knowledge
prepares us to face the
uncertain world, while
paving the way for technical
and artistic progress.

Expansion of consciousness
effortlessly dissolves the
ill feelings of envy, anger,
greed, egoism, and frustration.

The cycle of expansion
differentiates the one into
many and its reverse
assimilates all into the one.

...

Known

Discovery reveals that
which exists but is
not known.

Creativity uses the
known to make
something new.

We tend to memorize
the known, but by
knowing the principle,
the known is never
forgotten.

Probing the known
separates the fake and
imaginary known from
the real known.

Only those who have
mastered the known
seek the unknown.

...

Words

Language is essential for
remembering thoughts and
conforming to the world
we are born into.

Real thinking needs no
words, just as emotions
flow without them.

New insights arise without
words, and later, a new
language is invented
to express it.

All new equations of
science and mathematics
were written after gaining
an insight into a phenomenon
or a problem.

Words are useful for
remembering great ideas,
and for educating those who
lack insights and real thinking.

...

Glow of Silent Truths

Imitation

Imitation is a ladder of
progress; each step
leads to improvement.

Imitation is often the
instrument used in the
diffusion of technologies
and their uses.

We have a tendency to
imitate the practices
and systems that we
find successful.

Imitation is ingrained
in our genes, because
evolution favors those who
imitate the successful.

Various art forms get
refined through successive
imitation of previous works.

Setting an example for others
to imitate is the oldest and
most effective way of teaching.

...

Glow of Silent Truths

Reaction

All living beings react to external events and stimuli because reactions are biological impulses.

Application of intelligence confers the power of reasoning, which, in turn, limits the reactive responses.

Reactions not backed by reasoning are the source of most bad decisions and adverse outcomes in life.

Reactions arise from the material complexity of the organisms.

Reasoning over reactions raises the self above the compulsions of biological existence.

...

Release

Many joys of life come from
finding the release from
a stressful situation.

Many times we deliberately
get into a stressful situation
for feeling the thrill of
the release.

Watching a closely fought
game builds tension and
pleasure is in the release
at the end of the game.

There is a joy at the end of a
long wait, because it marks the
release of the stress of waiting.

A challenge at work creates
tension, and its execution
brings release, giving us
the pleasure of work.

We collect many things
in life to satisfy our desires,
but many joys are found in
releasing those accumulations.

…

Glow of Silent Truths

Shades of Truth

In our experience of the world,
truth appears to us in many shades,
like a spectrum of split light, but
never as one whole white light.

This is so because in this
relative world, knowing
the absolute truth is
beyond cognition.

Many experiences and objects
reveal shades of truth to us,
such as the awe-inspiring
beauty of nature.

We see a shade of the truth
when a work of art evokes
the same imagination with
which it was created.

Inspiration is a shade of the
truth, as is finding a solution
to a difficult problem.

A moment of epiphany or
feeling connected to the
world is a shade of truth.

...

Glow of Silent Truths

Timing

Ancient mathematics and
astronomy were developed
largely to get the timing
right for important events.

The popularity of many
beliefs and superstitions has
its source in the desire to
get the timing right.

Inspiration to act at a
particular instant is a
signal of correct timing.

Lucky people have the knack for
timing their actions correctly.

Timing of various functions in
the body creates biorhythms
making life possible.

Even time was invented in an
attempt to get the timing
right for the world affairs.

Timing in life is subtle
and key to success.

...

Glow of Silent Truths

Contradiction

Many things in the world
appear contradictory to us.

These contradictions arise
because of the bipolarity of
existence in which all objects
have their polar opposites.

All knowledge gained from
the reality of a bipolar world
inherits polar opposites.

Therefore we often find that
what we conclude about
something, the opposite of it
also turns out to be true.

Love comes with hate,
attention with distraction,
pleasure with pain, and
matter with anti-matter.

When we see both the
poles of the order of
existence we see it as
a contradiction.

...

Glow of Silent Truths

Self-assertion

Self-assertion is not
the same as egotism,
though the ego arises
from the self.

Self-assertion keeps
actions triggered by
volatile emotions
under check.

Feeble self-assertion is the
reason for the feelings of
hate, anger, or greed.

Setbacks in life subdue
the egoistic behavior
thereby creating space
for self-assertion.

Self-assertion infuses the
meaning, motivation, and
clarity of purpose into our
actions.

...

Glow of Silent Truths

Defensiveness

We are defensive when
we do not want to accept
our mistakes.

Blaming others for bad
outcomes is a common
sign of a defensive mindset.

We are defensive when we
know we are in the wrong,
but feel that being truthful
will cause a loss of face.

A defensive mindset compels
us to tell many lies, and each
lie makes us insecure.

Slowly, we start believing
in our own lies, making
it difficult for us to
learn and grow.

Antidote to defensiveness is
to take responsibility for
our actions, regardless of
the consequences.

...

Glow of Silent Truths

Discovery

We know the pleasure of
opening a present.

It is not so much the
things inside, but the
act of uncovering that
gives us the pleasure.

An act of uncovering
stirs hope, surprise,
and curiosity.

Scientists are driven on
the path of discovery,
without caring what
lies ahead.

Sages are on the journey of
the unknown hoping to
discover the ultimate truth.

We desire to be surprised
and hope to discover that
we search for, all the time,
not knowing what we seek.

...

Glow of Silent Truths

Cry

We may know how
a few things happen,
but it is hard to find
why they happen.

A baby cries out of hunger
but crying expands her
lungs for growth.

Is she crying out of
hunger or for the future?
we may say it is for both.

It is possible there is
another why;
it can be a cry of
becoming.

...

Glow of Silent Truths

Wave of Existence

The cosmos is a form of
vibrating energy.

It appears to us in
movement of stars and
galaxies, electrons
and photons.

This movement is
the elusive reality that
we seek unknowingly.

Yet, in the act of
knowing it, we interrupt
the movement.

Thus, we know only a
fragment of reality,
a freeze-frame of a
moving wave.

Existence is nothing
but movement,
an eternal wave
in motion.

...

Glow of Silent Truths

Pain

What is experienced is
pain, and suffering is
just a memory of it.

A true act of forgiving
cures suffering, for it
erases the memory of
the hurt.

Most people are
suffering not from pain,
but from an inability
to erase its memories.

Pain is sensorial and
subsides when the body
heals, while suffering
is a mental agony and
hard to overcome.

Pain is a part of living;
refusing to suffer is a choice
requiring a forgiving heart
and selective amnesia.

...

Glow of Silent Truths

The Tree

We rejoice on seeing
a tree, for we came
from the tree.

The tree gives its all,
out of love to us, as a
parent would to a baby.

The tree is also a remedy
for loneliness because
in it we may find the
joy of meeting our ancestor.

The trees are delightful,
for they nourish all
living beings and fill
their hearts with joy.

In the company of trees,
some have attained nirvana,
some discovered secrets of
nature, and some found
relief from their grief.

...

Glow of Silent Truths

Past

There is no unchanging
past, just as there is no
certain future.

The present keeps on
rewriting the past,
so memory of the past
changes with time.

The past is not the same as
what actually happened then;
it is as it is remembered
in the present.

The past will change in
the future, for memory of
those events will change.

Future discoveries and
values change the lens
on the past, like an
ever-changing kaleidoscope.

Let's not judge the past;
leave it where it belongs--in the past.

...

Glow of Silent Truths

Wheel of Karma

Sometimes we make huge gains
without much effort, at other
times our actions bear no fruit.

It is the manifested prior karma
that enables high rewards for
small efforts and renders
great struggles futile.

Manifested prior karma is the
initial condition of the present,
which combines with actions in
the present to shape the destiny.

Outcomes in line with efforts imply
lower load of the manifested karma.

When efforts bear little returns,
manifested karma is blocking the path.

When small steps result in big strides,
manifested karma is paving the way.

Actions not bearing results
get accumulated as karma
to manifest later.

...

Glow of Silent Truths

Nostalgia

Nostalgia makes the past seem
perfect, because the daily
grind of the present renders
the past feeling better than
it actually was.

Acts of camping, fishing and
hunting are remembered
fondly when sweat, toil, and
hardships are long forgotten.

Minor tussles of the past
appear as great acts of courage;
we vividly recall past moments
favorable to our self-esteem.

In most cases, the present is
better than the past and
future will be better
than the present.

As we age, we yearn
for the beautiful past.

In fact, this aching is
for lost youthfulness
and is known as nostalgia.

...

Glow of Silent Truths

Knowing

We know not what
we do not know.

Strangely, we also know not
what we do know.

Failure is caused by thinking that we
know something, but the outcome
shows we actually did not.

Every failure tells us
that we do not know what
we think we know.

Every success baffles us, as we
barely know how we achieved it.

Actually we knew it, but
did not know that we knew it.

Occasionally, something great is done
unknowingly, and we have a word
for such triumphs -- intuition.

Knowledge is knowing that
which we do not know;
we scarcely know what we do know.

...

Glow of Silent Truths

Opening

Solid metals do not let air
go through them, but
let current flow,
so, they are hollow
in a unique way.

An atom is mostly a void,
yet almost nothing can
go past it, though a neutrino
can go right through.

There are no barriers
in the world; some paths
are opaque, some clear,
everything has an opening.

The wall in front may
be a step to climb up,
and an open window,
a deceptive abyss.

The world is built this way.

...

Glow of Silent Truths

Transition

We mostly make sense of
transitions at the extremes,
as in the birth of the new
and the end of what was.

We are alarmed by the
sudden transitions and
often remain oblivious
to the gradual transitions.

Spring is a transition from
winter to summer and
lasts a few weeks.

Adolescence is a transition
from childhood to adulthood
spanning a decade.

Transitions to oblivion
span several years.

...

Glow of Silent Truths

Feedback

Much of the positive
feedback is flattery
and given by those
seeking favors.

A feedback for improvement in
our attitude, performance, or
appearance is likely to be acted
upon if it is without disdain.

Generally any direct
feedback is taken as
a criticism and is not
well received

Feedback that work is
usually given in jest or in
a subtle manner without
any trace of contempt.

Karma gives the best feedback
by granting bitter and sweet
fruits of the past actions.

...

Glow of Silent Truths

Interaction

Interactions are at the root of
all creations, evolutions,
and dissolutions.

Observation is also a form of
interaction, and every observation
changes the observed.

Our worldview develops through
participation in the interactions
over time, and there exists no
objective world for us to know.

Interaction of imagination and
action creates arts, science,
technology, and relationships.

Every interaction changes
the participants in some way,
and occasionally, an interaction
annihilates the participants.

…

Meditation

Any act that focuses the attention on one thought or object is a meditation.

Being fully absorbed in work is a meditation, and observing with intensity is a meditation.

Experiencing pleasures with mindfulness is a meditation, so is listening to sounds in silence.

Sitting at a quiet place is a meditation, so is a long walk.

Silencing the noise of speech, thought, and action is the reward of meditation, but only a few seek this reward.

...

Glow of Silent Truths

Disguised Truths

It is by design that the truths of existence are disguised.

A tree is hidden within its seed.

The conscious mind obscures the commands of the unconscious.

Rich resources are found buried in the depths of the earth.

Secrets of the world are coded in the equations.

Essence of all things is concealed; it requires considerable effort to uncover it.

Ironically, removing one veil reveals a truth only to expose another disguise.

...

Numbers

Numbers enable us to make better
sense of the things around us.

We understand warmth and coldness
better by assigning a number to each.

Emotions, works of art, and beliefs
remain partially understood
because they cannot be easily
converted into numbers.

Most research involve applying numbers
to attributes or phenomena and
studying the changes in numbers
for arriving at conclusions.

Knowledge defined by
numbers is at the root of the
progress of many technologies.

The certainty of numbers provides
comfort in an uncertain world.

...

Glow of Silent Truths

Attention

Those who benefit from our attention, often blame us for being distracted frequently.

Those in authority tend to deride us for our lack of attention span, as it implies defiance of their authority.

Smart attention seekers avoid wasting our scarce attention resource on long, drawn-out, and tedious details.

Algorithms on social media draw our attention by showing us what we want: amusement, simplified conclusions, and confirmation of our beliefs.

Modern gadgets make available what we want, but prevent us from wanting what we need.

...

Glow of Silent Truths

Control

Self-discipline consists of taking
the right actions without
any external control.

In a progressive society,
self-discipline is the norm
together with loosening of
controls imposed by traditional
beliefs and governments.

The ability to hide our
emotions and the ability to
control emotions are two
different things.

Those who need external
controls are novices,
and those who need no
controls are masters.

We often make a mess of
things when we try to
control them.

Therefore, the big decisions of
our lives are often beyond
our control.

...

Glow of Silent Truths

Infinite

Apart from mathematical infinity,
there are many other kinds of
infinities in the world.

There are infinities that are
unreachable, and others
that cannot be exceeded and
still others that defy measurement.

The sky evokes a sense of infinity
because it appears boundless.

The absolute zero temperature is
considered an infinity because
it cannot be reached.

The speed of light is infinite
because it cannot be surpassed.

Knowledge is infinite, as is ignorance.
Memory is infinite, as is intelligence.
Light is infinite, as is darkness.

Time is infinite, but we measure it
with our lives, so it becomes finite for us.

...

Glow of Silent Truths

Seeking Bliss

We spend most of our time
in pursuit of many
kinds of pleasures.

We are driven to seek
physical pleasures and
those that satisfy our ego.

Sensory pleasures are fleeting in nature,
while ego pleasures last much longer.

In fact, we are not chasing
transient pleasures of the world,
but seeking enduring bliss.

We know deep within
that such a bliss exists,
but we are unable to find it.

Therefore, we run after many pleasures
in the hope of finding the elusive bliss.

...

Virtue

Conforming to our innate
nature is normal while going
against it is a virtue.

Hypocrisy is natural to humans,
resisting it makes one noble.

As a survival strategy, deception is
encoded in all living beings;
choosing not to deceive is integrity.

Submitting to the strong is natural;
defiance of the strong is courage.

Lying to defend the strong is customary;
defending the truth is audacity.

Punishing the weak for disorder is common;
punishing the strong for deviance is justice.

Defending social norms and values is
without risk, while supporting
freedom of ideas is flirting with danger.

...

Prayer

We pray to the unknown,
for we know not why
or how our lives unfold.

Prayer is the source
of all faiths and an
affirmation of life itself.

Sometimes we pray
out of fear of losing what
we have: health, family,
wealth, and reputation.

Often, we pray to
gain what we lack:
health, family, wealth,
and reputation.

We direct the prayer
to the external, while
the center of prayer
lies within.

The true prayer is
to express gratitude
and show reverence
to existence.

...

Glow of Silent Truths

Manifested World

What is the need for
the manifested world
if the universe is full of
intelligence?

One possible answer is
that the manifested world
enables the universe to
become self-conscious.

At the moment of individual
awakening, the knower
and the knowledge unite
with the universe.

At that moment, the universe
experiences itself and the purpose of
the manifested world is fulfilled.

Very few of us reach the
moment of awakening
and enable the universe
to experience itself.

...

Glow of Silent Truths

Description

A thing described is
no longer what it really is,
because it is a simplification,
as in an outline.

The outline places details into
a black box, and we know not
what lies within.

Most descriptions are no
more than elaborate labeling,
naming a thing merely makes
a mental note of its existence.

Descriptions without
understanding are often
an exercise of a lazy mind.

The unknown has been described
as God, but we know so little
about the unknown.

Descriptions tend to fragment reality,
while it is the sum of all things.

...

Glow of Silent Truths

Search

If we search, we find something,
not necessarily what we set out to find.

Sometimes a great mystery unfolds,
and at times, a great secret is revealed.

A search never goes futile;
often we fail to notice the outcome.

The universe has this unique
quality of its self-revealing nature.

An external search reveals
the deep truth about the world
we live in.

If we embark on an inner search,
some aspect of the self
may become known.

We should always keep searching,
for the universe never stops
revealing itself.

...

Showing off

We often show-off to hide something,
lofty language to dress up
a self-evident idea.

Sometimes we display confidence
to cover nervousness as in walking
briskly, or we fake smiles to mask
sadness within.

Many of us show off big cars
to hide a petty heart, and
flashy clothes to hide
emptiness in life.

Some of us make noise about
the truth to hide lies,
while others make a display of
honesty to cover deceits.

Hiding noble deeds and
revealing selfish acts is
the beginning of the virtue.

...

Glow of Silent Truths

Tears

Tears in the eyes, smiles on face,
and spring in stride are the
signs of emotions flowing out.

But we have learnt to fake smiles and
walk briskly to show sham confidence.

However tears are hard to fake,
because tearful eyes are the
mirror to our hearts.

Welled-up eyes are not our
weaknesses, but a reminder of
being alive and real.

Tears signal real feelings
and faking them is fraught with risk,
as they may cause the fake emotion
to become real.

...

Interregnum

Interregnum incubates changes
and gives us a chance to
reorder our lives.

In the interregnum the nebulous new
order begins to take shape, though
the final form remains vague.

Things that move fast have short
interregnum, and slow moving
things have long interregnum.

Trends emerging in the interregnum
may last from a few seconds to
several years.

Paths to positive change can be found
by focusing on the interregnum of
events shaping our world.

Interregnum of our breaths is
the point of self-discovery.

...

Curiosity

Being curious is an
echo of self-consciousness,
for curiosity arises from a
call of the consciousness.

Curiosity is a quest for the
knowledge that transcends
our needs for survival.

All questions arise
out of curiosity, so all
progress is built on the
foundation of curiosity.

Sometimes risks arise
while satisfying curiosity,
so dangers are inherent
in chasing curiosity.

Cultivating curiosity makes
us authentic because
curiosity is hard to fake.

Devotion to curiosity
takes us on the path of
finding the purpose of life.

...

Glow of Silent Truths

Aspiration

The capacity to aspire is
a blessing, for it signifies
the freedom of choice.

The tendency to imitate
and the feeling of jealousy
confirm the presence of
aspirations.

Aspiration to dominate is
the reason for the abuse of
power by those who wield it.

New learnings ignite
fresh aspirations and
enable us to keep pace
with changing times.

We lose interest in trying
hard when the flames of
aspiration no longer
flicker.

...

Rare

Knowledge with humility and
information with secrecy are rare.

Triumph with modesty and
freedom without risk are rare.

Learning without failures and
focus without discipline are rare.

Growth without scarring and
success without luck are rare.

Patience without fretting and
justice without delay are rare.

Riches without excesses and
power without abuses are rare.

Wisdom without silence and
bravery without fear are rare.

...

Glow of Silent Truths

Danger

It is safe to know the truth
but making it public is
fraught with danger.

It is harmless to have
freedoms, but exercising
those freedoms is dangerous.

We may feel good about
criticizing the leaders of
a country, but criticizing
a local politician is
dangerous.

It is easy to rail against
bigotry but dangerous
to confront a bigot.

We are eloquent for
winning arguments from
the safety of distance, and
silent in the face of danger.

...

Glow of Silent Truths

Obligations

Obligations are rooted in the
idea of reciprocity, and
form the basis of morality.

Obligations are not compulsions,
for we always have a choice in
fulfilling obligations.

Obligations bind us to the past
and are a call for the return of
favors in the form of our duties
to our families and society.

We are an extension of the
past and it is the past that
imposes obligations on us.

Choosing not to discharge
obligations snaps the
continuity of the past and
disrupts the emergence of
the future.

...

Glow of Silent Truths

Prediction

Prophets and seers are
venerated for their ability
to predict the future.

Analysts are paid for their
intelligence in using statistical
tools to predict the
future trends.

Entrepreneurs who correctly
predict the future of businesses are
rewarded with success.

Apparently, the source of
veneration, intelligence, and
success is the ability to
predict the future.

Charlatans make all kinds of
predictions to their
own advantage.

It is preferable to make
our own predictions to
shape our future.

...

Innocence

Not reading hidden
motives in other's
actions is innocence.

Trusting those we
love is innocence.

Following advice given in
good faith is innocence.

Not cheating others for one's
own benefit is innocence.

Speaking less and listening
more is innocence.

Not making excuses for
failures is innocence.

Being grateful for
life is innocence.

Though there is a price to be
paid for being innocent,
retaining the innocence after
paying the price is greatness.

...

Glow of Silent Truths

Limits

Everything exists within its
limits of existence, beyond
which it loses its integrity
and essence.

All physical laws hold within
their limits, but social practices
devised by us often survive
beyond their limits, causing
many crises of our age.

Our thinking and perceptions
set limits on our imaginations.

We are aware of life within
the limits of birth and death,
because our consciousness has
been framed by these limits.

Knowing the limits of
the known makes the
knowledge complete.

...

Glow of Silent Truths

Experience

Experience is the
direct proof of
consciousness, and it is
the essence of living.

All experiences teach
us something.

Little things and small
gestures are full of
delightful experiences,
if we care to pay attention.

Pleasure lies in savoring the
moments and relishing
their lingering experience.

The purpose of some
experiences in life is to
reveal the secrets of
knowledge.

...

Unequal world

We own nothing in this world;
we keep finding and losing things
throughout our lifetime.

We get our body to live in it,
and emotions to experience.

Some gain big money for small
effort, others get little money
for big effort.

Some inherit a healthy body to live in,
while some get a body riddled
with afflictions.

Some have a family to fall
back upon, others have
no one to lean on.

Who is giving what we get,
why is it giving so
unequally ?

...

Glow of Silent Truths

God

Fear of nature and dread of
afterlife compel us to believe
in stories of gods.

A perceived answering presence
reinforces belief in God,
though not all prayers are
answered.

Authors of yore invented
many faiths around
unexplained marvels
and fables.

So, for most people,
God resides in the troika of
fear, magical tales, and
answered prayers.

Beyond beliefs, there is
a mystery that reveals
itself to a select few.

Connecting to this
mystery is the basis of
all spiritual experiences.

...

Glow of Silent Truths

Puzzle

Everything appears to be
random, until a pattern is
found within the chaos.

Randomness is a
coded puzzle; we need
to decode it to gain
insights from it.

There is randomness
within randomness;
deciphering one level
leads to the next.

Often, a solution fails
at the next level, showing
that the solution is false
for the second layer.

Randomness separates
the wise from the ordinary,
and the purpose of life is to
keep solving the puzzle.

...

Glow of Silent Truths

Void

There are photons
we see, and
waves we hear.

There are clusters of
atoms we touch, and
bundles of molecules
we taste.

There are things we smell,
and nothingness that we sense.

It is a light unseen, and
a sound unheard.

It is an aroma never smelled,
and a presence that is never
touched nor tasted.

It is that which
does all these things:
a void.

...

Glow of Silent Truths

Extinction

When something grows,
substratum decays;
when a thing is born,
something dies.

As a plant develops
soil degenerates;
a baby's birth take
a lot out of the mother.

Growth and decay
always happen together,
fast growth leads
to faster decay.

What is decaying in this
wild material progress
driven by inventions
and technology?

Perhaps life is being
sucked out of the planet,
and we may be marching
towards the extinction.

…

Glow of Silent Truths

Dreams

What happens when
we sleep, apparently,
we rest and reinvigorate
ourselves.

We also enter the realm
of the unconscious and
the world of dreams.

Some dreams are
recollections of the
past, while others may
foretell the future.

Let's be mindful of the
non-verbal dreams
that are full of images
and movements.

These may reveal
secrets of the past or
signpost the future.

...

Happiness

Happiness is fulfilment
of what we want, and
it rarely happens and
lasts only briefly.

So, we begin to search for
happiness in what we have:
in relationships, money
or our jobs.

We know that all efforts
to pursue happiness in
things end in some kind of
disappointment.

Happiness is not found
in things.

Pleasures we chase exist
only in fleeting moments
and then vanish.

Happiness is the absence of
anxiety and stress, and
above all, an acceptance of
life as it is.

...

Glow of Silent Truths

Time

Time always ticks away;
we do not know from where
it comes, nor where it goes.

Perhaps, time is just another
name of change.

We notice changes all
around us and measure
them in hours or days.

Growing up and aging are
merely changes in the body,
reckoned in years.

We observe the shifting of
the stars and calculate time
from these ever-changing patterns.

The seasons, the sun, and the moon
return quickly; many things
seem never to return.

So, it appears that some changes are
irreversible, but everything comes back
eventually in the cycle of time.

...

Glow of Silent Truths

Passionate Strivers

A select few people control
world affairs, steering it in
their wisdom and self-interests.

They frame the rules and
norms of the world, and
set the agenda for talks
and actions.

Some among them bend these
rules and norms at will,
considering themselves
above the rulebook of society.

The majority are strivers,
simply trying to survive
in the world,

Some lucky strivers with
passion for what they do,
sometimes join the select
few of the world.

...

Glow of Silent Truths

Poise of Mind

Our reactions to real or
imagined events are
mostly emotional.

Essentially, emotions are
involuntary, as they are
biological in nature.

Growing up often involves
learning to conceal emotions,
and this frequently leads
to mental stress.

True wisdom unfolds
when no emotion arises,
regardless of the events
around us.

This is poise of mind,
the highest state of
existence.

...

Glow of Silent Truths

Forests

Forests are unknown,
fearsome, and mysterious;
peaceful and violent;
and free from greed.

All weaklings exist in
the forest as food for the
strong and that is the
law of the forest.

Waterhole in the forest is
the most thrilling place;
visitors risk their lives
to drink the elixir,
and the drama of life
unfolds there.

The life-giving water is
accessible to only those
willing to risk life.

Those who avoid risk
out of fear remain
forever unsated.

...

Glow of Silent Truths

Restlessness

Restlessness commonly
indicates frustration and
disappointment with
life as it is.

Various relaxation
techniques are devices for
releasing the energy of
restlessness.

Being fully absorbed in a
task is a reliable way to
channel the energy of
restlessness into some
productive work.

Restlessness -- to travel, to
write, to do something --
can be an inspiration that is
knocking at our doors.

Sometimes restlessness of an
unknown nature troubles us;
it may be a sign of creative
potential building
up inside us.

...

Glow of Silent Truths

Message

We tend to extend the
message by reading that
which is not intended
or conveyed.

Optimists read good news
when it is absent in a message,
while pessimists read bad
news when it is not there.

Our state of mind influences
our reading, when the mind is
negatively disposed, a bad news
becomes the worst news through
mental amplification.

Reading properly saves
us from many anxieties
and disappointments.

We frequently miss
the messages coded
with opportunities
or risks.

...

Glow of Silent Truths

Trouble

We are troubled when
our expectations are
not met.

Our plans represent a
trajectory of expectations
for achieving goals;
when plans go awry at
any stage we are troubled.

If we are troubled by
a thought, it may be an
inspiration; if troubled
by money, it may be a call
to change our lifestyle.

If we are troubled by
worries then it's time to
change our thinking.

Troubles are those that
nudge us to change, and
not changing when in
trouble is the real trouble.
...

Glow of Silent Truths

Compulsion

Voluntary actions are free from
compulsions and are marked
by the freedom of choice.

Some involuntary actions stem
from the unconscious, and
others are forced by the
external compulsions.

Rarely do actions taken
under external compulsion
produce the desired outcomes.

Many noble or fatal deeds
are done without planning
or thinking because they are
driven by the unconscious.

Not deviating from the chosen
course of action despite
external compulsions is a
sign of freedom and courage.

This courage keeps us
on the right path.

...

Glow of Silent Truths

Principles

Purpose of principles adopted
in life is to protect our self-esteem
and to fit into the ecosystem in
which we survive and thrive.

Our ingrained biases and
the conveniences of living
challenge our adopted
principles every day.

To resolve this mental conflict,
we use self-serving reasons to
excuse our actions that are
contrary to our adopted principles.

Religious scriptures are very handy
in justifying our actions, as they
can often be read in a manner that
justifies almost any action.

Self-interest is the ruling principle,
which is seldom sacrificed
for adopted principles.

...

Glow of Silent Truths

Assumptions

Our known and unknown
assumptions enable us to
make sense of the world.

All learning is mostly
about imbibing a new
set of assumptions.

Our biases and irrational
thinking are grounded
in our assumptions, and
all misunderstandings
arise from them.

Self-mastery begins with
the critical examination of
our assumptions.

Upon reflection, we may identify
many assumptions, but
some remain forever unseen.

With assumptions, we can
only know transient truths,
because absolute truth is
free from assumptions.

...

Glow of Silent Truths

Talent

All of us are born with the talent
needed to live as human beings,
but some are born with special talents
to achieve great successes in life.

Those destined for great
accomplishments possess
the talents required to
succeed in their time.

Many talents are not
recognized as talents
due to a lack of avenues
for expression.

Not long ago, playing a
game was merely recreation,
but now, talent in sports, is
valued more than talent
in science or art.

Having the talent needed in
the present is rewarding, but
nature also nurtures talents
needed in the future.

...

Glow of Silent Truths

Anarchy

Anarchy is not lawlessness,
as it is commonly understood;
anarchy is the absence of
authority for regulating freedoms.

Anarchy is an utopia where
self-regulation is the rule, and
individuals, while enjoying their
freedoms, do not harm anyone.

The purpose of all authorities is
to restrict the freedoms,
because many people often
misuse their freedoms.

The potential of human creativity and
imagination has found expression
in the sphere of arts because
authorities are permissive of
anarchy within the arts.

Freedoms always carry the
risk of anarchy, and those who
favor authority over anarchy
actually fear freedom.

...

Glow of Silent Truths

Renunciation

Renouncing pride creates
space for wisdom to fill it, and
renunciation of negative thoughts
makes the mind composed.

Indifference to likes and
dislikes is the beginning of
renunciation.

Renunciation matures
with waning of desires
and non-attachment to
possessions.

Renunciation of emotions,
relationships, and knowledge is
harder than renunciation of
money and power.

True renunciation eludes
us, when we hold on to our
possessions even after
giving them up.

...

Stranger

We trust a stranger
more than a friend in
revealing our deep secrets.

Anyone who conflicts with
our interests is an enemy;
a stranger is too distant
to pose a threat to
our interests.

Our friends may be
potential enemies,
but strangers are
potential friends.

We are stranger to our
own thoughts; we are
often astonished to find
rare wisdom in us.

Let's be like strangers
in a relationship for
its continuation.

...

Glow of Silent Truths

Pretense

Showing the best of ourselves is
not a pretense, for we are
using parts of our personality
to meet the need.

Pretense is in imitating
others as an impostor;
it is hiding our true selves.

Pretense is a valuable tool
to understand what we
lack and value.

Making a mental note of
what we pretend and
striving to acquire it makes
pretending useful.

In this world, success
will not come from simply
being who we are.

...

Glow of Silent Truths

Unconscious

The unconscious runs
all the routines of living,
and projects its decisions
onto the conscious to trick us
into believing that we are in
control of ourselves.

It allows the conscious to
take limited actions for
assessing external signals
to calibrate its responses.

Swinging between optimism
and pessimism is a drill of
the unconscious mind.

By doing this, the unconscious is
preparing us to deal with
the vagaries of life.

The unconscious is the real boss;
we know not whom we
serve all our life.

...

Glow of Silent Truths

Objective Reality

Is there an objective
reality and what is
its nature?

This search is at the crux
inquiry for seekers in both
science and spirituality.

Our conscious existence suggests
that there is something, though
its nature remains elusive.

Both consciousness
and matter exist and
interact within space.

The space inflates and
deflates on its own and
contains all.

Thus making space a
reflection of objective reality,
if not the objective reality itself.

We are contained within
objective reality and will
dissolve into it.

...

Glow of Silent Truths

Fear

Fear is born in
darkness of hatred
and feeds on
fog of uncertainty.

Fear is the source of
all mental agony,
breeding suspicion in life.

It makes us insecure in
relationships and clouds
our judgment at work.

Fear gnaws at
self-confidence,
wilting our resolve
to face adversity.

Fear is nothing
but an imagined
gremlin of childhood;
we can shrug it off
if we so choose.

...

Glow of Silent Truths

Expectation

We expect to be
loved and trusted.

We expect to be
rewarded generously
for the little work we do.

We expect our wrongs
to be ignored and
offenses to be forgiven.

We expect to be
admired for our looks,
attitude, and intelligence.

Are we willing to return
all that to others that we
expect from others?

...

Glow of Silent Truths

Trust

Trust is the best
antidote to worry;
trust gives us more
than it takes.

Fear and trust
cannot exist together,
we fear what we
do not trust.

The uncertainties of life are
the cause of anxiety,
and trust empowers us
to deal with them.

In durable relationships,
trust always trumps love.

Trust is really about self-belief,
and not about belief in others.

…

Glow of Silent Truths

Darkness

Darkness is not just when
we cannot see;
both light and lack of it
can be dark to us.

Some truths seem
dark to us because
we do not want to
see them.

What is seen without
eyes is visible
without being seen,
for it is the self.

Most of the world is
dark to us, the absence of
inner light spawns
this darkness.

Radiance within makes us
one with the world, but
destroys our identity.

...

Glow of Silent Truths

Sky

We like to look up rather
than down because we
grow up, not down.

We can be anywhere
on the globe; the sky is
always up there.

The notions of
'up' and 'down' are
our imagination, for the
sky is everywhere.

The sky wraps around
us like a tent and it is
also within us.

The sky is the one thing
that exists for sure;
we are not sure about
anything else.

...

Renewal

Anything that enters our
homes has the potential
to shift the balance of life.

We find ourselves in
an uplifting mood
when we bring home
a flowering plant.

Arrival of a baby changes
our fortune;
a new gadget opens
new vistas.

Even rearranging pieces
of furniture can be a
source of happiness.

Renewal is the universal
principle; sometimes,
little things can be
life-changing.

...

Glow of Silent Truths

Promise

Promise provides comfort
for risking our emotions and
wealth, and for keeping our
hopes alive for the future.

Money and commerce have
grown exponentially with the
promise of paper currency,
and now, that promises ride
on virtual codes.

All relationships and
transactions rest on
promises, thus, any breach
of a promise is either
a crime or a moral failing.

Promises carry a double
burden: the unknown future,
and the reliance on another's
ability to fulfill them.

Promises of great fortunes
in the distant future are often
made to deceive us.

...

Glow of Silent Truths

Stress

Stress that distracts is
negative, while the stress
that sharpens our focus
is beneficial.

If we are stressed
about the outcomes of
our actions, then it is
avoidable stress.

If we are stressed about
opinions of others, then
we are ceding control of
our lives to others.

If we are stressed about
taking the action that is
right for us, then it is a
catalyst for success.

Before a big success,
we often endure a great
stress, whereas those who
succeed without stress
do not find the success
as sweet or enduring.

...

Glow of Silent Truths

Center

Everything has a center
around which it is
formed and exists.

Asymmetric entities have
more than one center
and are therefore
wobbly.

Finding the center of a
phenomenon reveals its
essence and leads to
control over it.

So far, the center of the
quantum phenomenon
has eluded scientists,
so it remains a mystery.

We can control the mind,
if we can locate its center;
finding the center of our
being is nirvana.

...

Glow of Silent Truths

Moments

Life moves quickly
moment by moment;
not being present in the
moments is the reason for
missed opportunities.

Every moment comes
with two choices: we
can either let the
moment pass or act
in the moment.

We tend to latch onto
the moments that
conform to our mindset;
in a neutral state of mind,
moments slip past us.

With a negative attitude
we seize adverse moments,
and with a positive attitude,
we grasp the moments of
delight and creativity.

...

Glow of Silent Truths

Schemer

A successful person
without humility and
kindness is probably
a schemer.

Many of us are choosing
the path of duplicity for quick
gains in wealth and power,
thereby debasing ourselves.

This devious approach is
at the root of many of
the world's troubles.

Success built with dedication to
excellence in actions is not only
enduring, but it also makes
us kind, humble and wise.

Such actions often
contribute to making
the world a better place.

...

Glow of Silent Truths

Transient Truths

All of our truths are
limited by the conditions
in which they exist, but the
conditions change continuously,
rendering the truths transient.

Conditions under which a
truth ceases to be true form
its shadow.

Within that shadow,
all lies thrive.

Furthermore, occasionally
conditions change so
drastically that the lies
turn into the truths.

The world is a shadow of
eternal truth, and therefore
every worldly truth is
transient, like a shadow.

We mostly live in delusions
because we hold on to
our transient truths.

...

Glow of Silent Truths

Reflections

We mostly use reflections
to confirm our beliefs.

However, when we use it to
question our beliefs, we
develop new perspectives.

All stories and histories are
echoes of the reflections
of our ancestors.

An event is meaningful to
us when it finds reflection
in our memories and
impressions.

We may reflect a positive
or a negative meaning for
the same situation, depending
on our recall of past experiences.

Thinking is akin to
a beam of light, reflecting from
various surfaces, creating
a meaningful pattern for
actions or conclusions.

...

Glow of Silent Truths

Revenge

Revenge is a kind of
rebalancing act for the
harm done to us.

Revenge can never undo
the harm done, and may
actually hurt those who
take it.

When we feel wronged,
we often take revenge
on ourselves by reneging
on our beliefs or sulking.

Revenge does not give us
the closure we seek, as
we often do not know
the real force behind
the harm done to us.

Only rarely does
revenge reward us with
the end we desire.

...

Glow of Silent Truths

Watch

We are told that a watch
keeps time, but actually,
the watch and its extension--
the calendar-- are the scales
to measure our age.

These devices tell us
how much time we
have spent to this
very day and hour.

We can use a watch
to know for how long
we have been idling,
sulking, and complaining.

A watch is not essential
for sitting in silence and
observing time tick away.

The watch can truly be
a keeper of time only if
it can tell us how much
time remains for us.

...

Glow of Silent Truths

Cage

Occasionally, it appears
that we are inside a cage;
some call it the matrix.

Only a few wish to break
free from the cage.

The cage takes away our
freedoms and provides
food and safety, while
we seek elusive happiness.

Often, in search of happiness,
we add new layers to the
cage, thereby fortifying it.

We realize very late in life
that there is no happiness
without freedom.

Overcoming the mental
conditioning that created
the cage leads to freedom
and happiness.

...

Glow of Silent Truths

Possession

We desire a thing
until we obtain it;
owning that thing
cures its desire.

Things hard to obtain
are intensely desired
and seem inadequate
in offering fulfilment.

Often, we regret having
coveted a thing but still
find it difficult to let
go out of vanity.

Our craving for new
things is never-ending,
despite failing to get
the contentment
we seek.

Indeed, most of the
pleasures are in the
possession of things,
not in the things
themselves.

...

Glow of Silent Truths

Secret

Secret gives an advantage
to the holder, but on
pressing that advantage
the secret is lost.

Source of power is
to leverage the secret
without revealing it.

Only some people are
able to keep secrets,
but those secrets are
lost forever.

There is the deep
secret of death;
the moment we know it,
we cannot tell.

The best-kept secrets
are secret; nobody knows
that such secrets exist.

...

Glow of Silent Truths

Abundance

The universe holds
abundance of everything:
destruction and creation,
joy and grief.

We are enveloped by
the vastness of space,
innumerable galaxies
and stars.

There is an abundance of
rarity, where no two
things are the same.

Each raindrop is exceptional,
every snowflake is unique.

In this abundant universe,
each of us is an
extraordinary being.

...

Silence

Silence is a wonderful gift to us;
it makes our thoughts
clear and our insights sharp.

We have no choice but
to see, hear, and smell,
we have a choice to
remain silent.

We know so little about
everything around us,
so it makes sense to
observe silence.

Silence provides us with
extra time for making
better judgments
and choices.

Real silence is when
thoughts subside, and
peace descends upon us.

...

Glow of Silent Truths

Anger

Anger is a signal to the
world that we have
yielded to a situation.

We are often angry
because we cannot face
the world as it is.

Anger is an admission that,
in the unfolding situation,
we are unable to find our way.

Often, anger arises when our
expectations of others
and ourselves remain unmet.

Sometimes, in anger we say
what we have wanted to
say all along.

We are angry because we
do not know what to do,
but our ego refuses to
accept this truth, so it
makes us angry.

...

Glow of Silent Truths

Beauty

Beauty lies in the symmetry of
things and in the asymmetric
things with symmetry.

Mathematics is the most
symmetrical of all things,
so it has its unique beauty.

Complementarity carries
its inherent beauty; it is
seen when two contrasts
snugly fit into each other.

Thus, we have the beauty of
black with white and of
a glowing light in
engulfing darkness.

Anything that fills us
with joy is beautiful.

Beauty is all around us;
it is just that we have not yet
discovered it in all things.

…

Glow of Silent Truths

Envy

We have no control over
our feelings; we are envious
even when we try not to be.

Envy runs high when we feel
small and left behind;
we show off to provoke envy,
since it feels like the best compliment.

It arises when we see
the possessions of others,
things that we fancy, or even
things we own with pride.

Envy can inspire us
to strive harder,
to catch up with
those we feel matter.

A bruised ego is
the cause of envy,
and a large ego is
easily poked.

...

Glow of Silent Truths

Freedom

Every living being is born with
the freedom to imagine,
think, and act.

These freedoms are curtailed
by the biological limits
and the social norms.

For the continuation of
the existing order, societies
find ways to curb freedoms.

Because it is tough to go
beyond the conditioning of
upbringing, only a few are
able to fully enjoy these freedoms.

Those who yearn for freedom
from the social norms and
beliefs become dissenters,
rebels, ascetics, or prophets.

Often, free persons are seen as
dangerous, so enjoying natural
freedoms is filled with risks.

...

Glow of Silent Truths

Boundary

Every change involves crossing a
boundary, and it may be a
mental or physical frontier.

All obstacles are simply boundaries
that we must breach to continue
the journey.

When we step out of our home
or emerge from the womb,
we cross a boundary.

Some boundaries allow only
a one-way passage; once crossed
the door is shut behind us.

All discoveries of science
push the boundary, changing
our understanding forever.

Whenever a boundary is crossed,
a new world opens up before us.

...

Glow of Silent Truths

Imagination

All our dreams are
imaginations of the
past and the future
woven together.

Thinking is logical
imagination, while
imagination is
incoherent thought.

We should let
imagination define the
goal, and use thinking
to achieve it.

Imagining the impossible
makes it possible for
the great discoveries
to be made.

All imaginations are
potential possibilities;
impossible is simply that
which has not yet been
imagined.

...

Glow of Silent Truths

Thinking

Thinking is a conversation with ourselves;
while it occurs within the conscious mind,
it is stimulated by the unconscious.

There are more connections
for carrying information from
heart and gut to brain than
from the brain to the heart
and the gut.

This makes thinking a
function not only of the
brain, but also of the gut
and the heart.

Therefore, outcomes of our
thinking depend on food,
stress, environment, emotions
and various unknowns.

When thinking about
important issues it may be
sensible to consider them
in diverse settings over many days
before making a decision.

...

Indifference

Indifference to likes and
dislikes is a mark of a
composed mind and such
a mind is the source of
inner happiness.

Indifference to actions within our
control causes many sufferings,
while indifference to their
outcomes is wisdom.

An attitude of indifference
begins to take shape, as the ability
to control cravings and
emotional outbursts develops.

Zen-like indifference takes
root when impulses rise
with our consent.

...

Glow of Silent Truths

Wronged

Anyone who wrongs us is
not an agent, but a messenger;
therefore, it is better to bear the
pains and losses without ill will.

By reflecting on why someone
wronged us, we may discover that
we might have taken the same
action in the same situation.

When wronged by someone
we may think about the
harm as a correction in
the trajectory of life.

With this attitude, we can
avoid the feeling of revenge
against the agent of harm
and break the cycle of being
subjected to wrong again.

Forgiving is much easier if
we treat the agents of wrong
as messengers of bad news.

...

Glow of Silent Truths

Attraction

Often, we are attracted to the
things that we lack in life.

Some attractions arise
from biological needs,
some from desires for comfort,
and many from envy.

Attraction springs from
desires, but soon the
gratification wanes, and we
lose interest in the things
we were attracted to.

Rather than chasing the
things we are attracted to
we should have something
that attracts the things
we want.

Most things in the
material world are
attracted to money,
but money also attracts
what we detest.

...

Flow

The flow keeps water
fresh, causes the wind to
blow, makes the seasons
change and sustains life.

Everything that exists
flows, and things that
do not flow are illusions.

There is a flow of energy
within every substance,
shadows and darkness are
unreal since nothing
flows within them.

Imagination and memory
are creations of a flowing
mind within a body in a
flow, and creativity is
new ideas flowing out.

Existence is the flow of
energy, time, and space,
while differentiations arise
from the intersection of
these flows.

...

Glow of Silent Truths

Opportunity

Some choices in life open
doors of opportunity, and
some shut the doors.

Opportunity knocks on
the doors of everyone,
but only those prepared are
able to seize it.

A great opportunity is often
preceded by tempting
options to deflect us
toward easy paths.

Opportunities that appear
low-risk and require no
preparation are often
laden with the high risk of
stalling our progress.

Often, the opportunity of
unknown and uncertain
rewards leads us on
the right path.

...

Glow of Silent Truths

Playfulness

Festivals and rituals,
carnivals and fairs,
sports and parties are
cultural devices to make
us playful.

The joy of playfulness in
dancing and singing,
walking and wandering,
cooking and cleaning,
gardening and driving
makes life lively.

For playfulness lightens the
burdens of life, and fortifies us
to bear the pain free from suffering.

Playfulness is a source of
optimism and a way of
countering the weight of ego.

Apparently, there is no reason
for the world to exist other
than it being an expression of
playfulness.

...

Glow of Silent Truths

Defeat

We often discover that
defeats are blows aimed
at our egos and we win
when our intents are freed
from feeding it.

The cosmic intelligence
rarely rewards us
with the outcomes
that inflate our ego.

But we tend to weave
stories from the favorable
outcomes in life to
project our egos.

Being smug in success is
the early warning of
a coming defeat.

Our efforts begin to bear
fruit in life when we
defeat the ego.

...

Glow of Silent Truths

Inefficiency

The nature sustains itself
not only through efficiency,
but also by using inefficiency
to regulate runaway systems.

A virus that spreads rapidly is not
lethal to its hosts, and a deadly
virus spreads slowly, thus,
inefficiency in virus preserves life.

Market inefficiencies allow
products and firms to survive
longer, thereby safeguarding
jobs and incomes for those
dependent on them.

A tyrant often fails to completely
suppress opposition because the
inefficiency of the military and
bureaucracy enables resistance
to endure and eventually
overthrow the dictator.

Inefficiency prolongs the
continuity of species, lifespans,
and institutions by providing a
second chance for survival.

...

Glow of Silent Truths

Compass

Having a compass and
occasionally reading it
provides a reality check
on orientation of a journey.

A compass points out the
direction in which we are
traveling, but it never tells
us the direction in which
we ought to travel.

Self-reflection is the
compass for knowing
the direction of life's
journey.

This unique compass also
points out where we
ought to be going in
our lives.

...

Glow of Silent Truths

Hate

Things that we hate
are attracted to us,
hate is the reason for
bad outcomes in life.

We hate adversity, poverty,
ill health, and failures
and end up inviting
these troubles in our life.

Force of attraction of the
things we abhor is in
proportion to the
degree of hate.

Objects of desire elude
us most of the time
because our cravings
drive them away.

The universal law is that
hate attracts, and
cravings repel.

Shunning the extremes of hate
or longing, and staying near
the middle, makes life fulfilling.

...

Glow of Silent Truths

Inspiration

All great changes and
feats are the results of
inspired thoughts and
actions.

We all get inspiring thoughts
and ideas to enrich our lives
and find our purpose.

Often we fail to recognize
the signals of inspired thinking
and miss opportunities to
transform our lives.

Out of habit, we disregard
many impulsive thoughts.

A recurring thought,
a vision of the future and
a feeling of restlessness
are signals of inspiration.

Inspiration is a message
from the future; it arrives
to shape the present for
that future.

...

Glow of Silent Truths

Win

All wins are temporary;
only striving to win is
permanent.

Life itself is a win, but
it is transient, as are
all wins of life.

We are winning even
when we are losing only
if we keep trying with
enthusiasm.

After each win we
have to start afresh,
winning never allows
us to take a respite.

Winning without the
desire for victory is
a noble win.

...

Glow of Silent Truths

Attachment

Investing time, emotions,
and money fixes the mind
on things and ideas.

This fixation of mind causes
attachment and our ego
kicks in to preserve it.

The ego begins to
establish ownership and
thus becomes burdened
with ideas and things.

Strangely, we hold on to
our dislikes more than
we do to our likes.

Attachment is a burden
on our ego, and purging
dislikes is an easy way
to unburden it.

...

Success

Externally success is
about fame and money;
internally it is about
learning and evolution.

Every success has seeds of
failure, and success is often
built on a foundation of failures.

The failures that follow
success, prepare us for
the next level of success.

Often the external success
comes at the cost of inner
peace, family, and health.

There are no failures in life,
if the definition of success is
becoming better at what
we do.

...

Risk

We do not easily recognize
risks, as our reflex actions
take care of many risks.

We underestimate the
risks of living and overestimate
our ability to manage them.

We mostly notice risk in
hindsight, after narrowly
escaping from an adverse
outcome.

In fact, every situation
subtly suggests the
possibility of many
adverse outcomes.

We face the risk of
annihilation every
moment, and our
continuous survival is
the greatest of miracles.

...

Light

In the void of darkness,
sparks of light created
the universe.

Light carries all
information and energy;
all that exists is just a
show of light.

Light arises from
darkness, subsists and
dissolves into the
darkness.

The darkness wills to
become the universe,
and light emanates
from its fold.

Perhaps the eternal
darkness is the source of
consciousness we keep
searching for.

...

Glow of Silent Truths

Acceptance

Often, we do not easily
accept what is assigned
to us in life.

Because what we get is
either less than our
expectations or completely
contrary to our wishes.

Mental resistance to
accepting life's servings is
the cause of an anxious life.

Acceptance of losses,
insults, and afflictions
builds the inner resilience
to face these challenges.

Acceptance leads to
changes we seek in our
life and makes it livable.

...

Glow of Silent Truths

Moment of Truth

When the truth becomes known,
the questions subside, and
life's dilemmas dissolve.

In the perception of
the whole truth,
nothing remains
unknown.

When the whole truth is
before us, we can readily find
answers to all the questions
that bother us in life.

At that moment, there may
be no need to seek
answers, as all questions
appear trivial.

Furthermore, there are
neither questions nor the
language to frame answers.

The search concludes with
the discovery that the
wisdom of silence is the
answer to all doubts.

...

Glow of Silent Truths

Politics

Every assembly of people is
political in nature, be it
a family, a club, or any other
form of grouping.

Togetherness for a common
purpose creates its own dynamics,
which we call politics.

Political power is often
captured and retained
through any means.

Disapproval of politics for the
use of unfair means reflects our
moral values, while the practice of
politics itself is neutral to both
fair and foul means.

The natural law of politics is
to follow ethics when it is
useful and disregard them
when necessary.

...

Glow of Silent Truths

Exit

We seldom enter a
relationship, a business venture,
or a job with an exit plan.

However, in hindsight,
we realize it would have been
useful to consider our exit options
before committing to any course of action.

Perhaps we feel entering is a
positive decision, while exit has
a negative connotation.

Entering may or may not
make life enjoyable, but
exiting provides immediate
release from stress or pain.

Exit is about removing the
thorns from our lives and
freeing us from the
mental and material traps.

The final exit ends both
the joy and pain of living.

...

Compromise

Survival in this harsh
world requires compromises.

And those who do not
submit to the demands of living
often shorten their lifespans.

Survival often demands
not defying the powerful,
taking actions against our
wishes, and dealing with
life's unfairness day after day.

Feeling of compromise is
a product of our ego;
it arises from refusing to
grasp the reality of life.

Accepting this reality saves
us from the frustrations
that we feel when making
compromises.

...

Glow of Silent Truths

Timeless

Space and time are two
poles of every entity;
without space there is
no time and without
time there is no space.

Everything that exists in
space is bound by time,
a timeless entity exists
beyond spatial dimensions.

Time differentiates space
into a multitude of things:
energy and matter,
elements and particles,
galaxies and stars.

Subtle entities are closest
to being timeless because
their spatial dimensions are
vanishingly small.

This is the reason that the
memories feel timeless to
us because they exist in a
very small crevice of brain.

...

Glow of Silent Truths

False Knowledge

Knowledge that shackles us to
beliefs is false.

Knowledge that claims a monopoly
over truth is false.

Knowledge that refuses
to answer questions is false.

Knowledge that forbids verification of
its assertions is false.

Knowledge that preaches tolerance of
the intolerants is false.

Knowledge that gives primacy to
authority is false.

Knowledge that instills
fear is false.

Knowledge that denies
freedoms is false.

Knowing what is false is a
path to knowledge.

...

Glow of Silent Truths

Oppression

A trauma, a tragedy,
a failure, or denied
wishes create a sense of
personal victimhood,
but it is not oppression.

In oppression there is
a widespread, systemic
approach, and it is often
impersonal.

Oppression deploys
ideologies, cultural norms,
and violent means to curb
freedoms and targets ability of
critical thinking.

We are at the deepest
end of oppression, when
we do not even know that
we are oppressed.

Discovering the ability to
identify the causes and
agents of oppression is the
beginning of liberation
from the oppression.

...

Glow of Silent Truths

Rise and Fall

The entire universe is a
display of energy waves,
and all waves by their very
nature rise and fall.

Thus, in our experience too,
we observe that what goes
up comes down and what
goes down comes up.

Everything in the world is
encoded to behave like
a wave, rising and falling
in succession endlessly.

We do not know when and
how we will rise or fall,
causing hopes and
fears in our lives.

Our feelings tend to
swing with the waves
of energy falling and
rising ceaselessly.

...

Glow of Silent Truths

Living in the Moment

Living in the moment means
remaining cheerful and positive,
even when nothing particularly
exciting is happening in our lives.

It means being composed
when things go wrong and
not being conceited when
things work out for us.

Doing the chores of living
without demur and
going about our duties
without whining are signs
of living in the moment.

Feeling emotions,
enduring pains, enjoying the
servings of life, and being
hopeful make for a life
lived in the moment.

Those who live in the
moment make life better
for others in some way,
and often leave behind
lasting accomplishments.

...

Glow of Silent Truths

Distraction

Distraction is a knock
on the door, or the ringing of
the phone while we are
sleeping, eating, reading
or doing our chores.

Anything that interrupts a train of
thought is a distraction,
often, distractions are useful,
as in stopping negative thoughts
or day dreaming.

Distractions are valuable in saving us
from unpleasant situations and
ending the weariness of living.

Often, distractions enable us to
rearrange our thoughts and
reach better answers, but occasionally
distractions may impede a new idea.

Some people wait endlessly for
distractions to spice up their lives,
while others whine about them.

...

Glow of Silent Truths

Choice

Every moment of life
offers us choices and our
actions of choosing are
the karma of the present.

Choices we make often
lead to unexpected results,
due to the complex interplay of
previous choices.

Choices we make in
life can be impulsive or
reasoned, but mostly we
take impulsive actions for
evading the exertions of
reasoning.

In times of crises, impulsive
choices may be useful, but
often they cause mental
agitation and anxiety.

The central message of the
karma theory is to follow
the path of excellence in
action, founded on
reasoned choice.

...

Glow of Silent Truths

Horizon

Many things in life are
like the horizon, always
there but unattainable,
while goals accomplished
disappear from the horizon.

Horizon is not real but
it can be seen, thus things
that can be observed are
not necessarily real.

In daylight horizon is far
away, but as darkness
gathers, the horizon
seems to close in on us,
eventually it envelops us.

Like the horizon, the
unrealized dreams of
life sometimes come to
us on their own, though
we often fail to notice
this miracle.

...

Glow of Silent Truths

Dimensions

Knowing a secret gives an
advantage in furthering our
interests, for it is like having
an extra dimension of information.

Observing from a height
gives an advantage as we
can see farther; thus, even an
extension of a dimension
comes with benefits.

It is conceivable that
all geniuses possess some
unknown extra dimension
that confers the intuitive
power and insights necessary
for creativity and discoveries.

Having an extra dimension
grants exceptional powers in
a world of lesser dimensions.

Three-dimensional creatures
would appear divine to two-
dimensional beings.

...

Glow of Silent Truths

Anchor

Our family and culture are
the anchor to which
we are tethered.

Similarly, society, religion,
and nation are anchors to
which we are tied.

Many anchors are devices
to fool us into believing
that we have freedom
without having one.

Only a few can escape
their anchors; the rest of
us yearn for freedom, while
carrying their chains.

The key to achieving
freedom is to break
free from anchors, while
retaining the bonds that
make us free.

...

Glow of Silent Truths

Walking

Walking gets rid of
mental stress and aids
in discovering inner peace.

Walking enables us to gain
new insights on problems
and to receive fresh ideas.

Walking is a remedy
for keeping the body
healthy and unburdening
the mind.

We should walk away
from the toxic relationships,
bad jobs, and rude people.

Walking is a great
gift to us, much like
silence, for leading
a joyful life.

...

Comparison

Without conscious awareness,
we often live in comparison
to something.

Comparison is a measuring
scale of achievements in
life, and often a source of
jealousy.

External comparisons
cause anxiety, anger,
and frustration.

However, comparison is
valuable when our own
progress is measured
over time.

Living without comparison is
the secret of a joyful life,
because comparison decides
winners mostly in sports.

...

Glow of Silent Truths

Discipline

Discipline is not just
following a time schedule,
or sticking to a routine

What we often mistake for
discipline is no more than
a dedication to habits.

We prefer discipline of habits
and routines, because it does
not require mental focus
and effort.

True discipline consists of
taking mindful and
steady actions towards
a definite goal.

The highest degree of
discipline is to keep the
mind under conscious
control at all times.

...

Art

Art is created when
we are so engrossed
in our actions that we
lose all sense of time.

Art is born when the
consciousness becomes
the action, and there is no
separate existence from
the act of creation.

We have a limited
definition of art,
often confined to
traditional forms,
so most works of art
remain unknown.

Thinking is an art, as
much as drawing a
painting or carving
a sculpture.

All inspired efforts
that give us joy and
purpose in living are
works of art.

...

Glow of Silent Truths

Signs

The vibes that we sense
whether positive or
negative are signs
emanating from
the universe.

These signs prepare us
for receiving good or
bad that is about to
befall on us.

Before life-transforming
events we get good
vibes and start feeling
better for no obvious reason.

We must not undermine
the positive signs with our
ingratitude or egotism.

A positive outlook in life
lessens the impact of
adversity and amplifies
the glad tidings.

...

Colors

The existence of the
universe perhaps needs
just two colors: black
and white; but many
colors exist.

Maybe the purpose of
these many colors is
to add to the beauty of
the creation.

We mirror the
many colors of
our colorful world.

We have many languages,
dances, dresses and foods--
so why can't we have
as many belief systems?

This immense diversity is a
constant reminder to us that
the beauty of existence is
in its many colors.

...

Glow of Silent Truths

Aroma

Aroma has the power
to lift our mood, and
it is aroma that makes
food taste great.

Long forgotten names
and places flash into
memory with their
associated aroma.

What we like is coupled
with a pleasant aroma
and what we dislike is
a stench to us.

Every significant event
of our life bears a unique
signature of aroma.

Aroma is the most
subtle of our senses;
it may one day unlock
the secrets of memory.

...

Glow of Silent Truths

Identity

We define our identity through
externalities: parents, gender,
faith, nativity, geography,
and skin color.

In all these aspects, we have
no choice; these are inherited
labels of the identity.

Identity can offer certain advantages
for survival, but more often, it is
used for limiting our freedoms.

Change-makers have never been
shackled by their inherited identities
when forging their own.

There are many who use their inherited
identities for projecting victimhood
and seeking entitlement.

The discovery of the identity without
any external reference is the final
discovery of the self.

...

Glow of Silent Truths

Space

Space has a dual
nature, appearing as
a wave or a particle
depending on how
it is observed.

We may think of space as a
continuum without attributes,
yet, it occasionally condenses in
some places into particles or
waves with properties.

When a particle is broken down
to its ultimate constituents,
what remains is only
the nothingness of space.

All we find is the infinite
space around us,
the prevalence of nothingness.

We are a condensed, minuscule
part of infinite space;
it is impossible for us to
fathom the infinite.

...

Glow of Silent Truths

Mountains

Mountains reflect many
colors and come in
myriad shapes.

They host lakes and glaciers,
trees and snow, and sometimes
spew melted rocks and fire.

Mountains are the refuge of
those who run away--in
search of freedom, or from
a coercive state, or from
an oppressive society.

Mountains make their
inhabitants resilient,
conferring them the
toughness to survive
in hard climes.

In the past people fled to
mountains to protect their
way of life, and now they rush
to them to escape the
heat of the world they live in.

...

Glow of Silent Truths

Mystery of Truth

Light is a particle and a wave
and what we perceive is neither,
we only see existence.

It is neither a particle nor
a wave, it is a part of the
elusive truth that we seek
to fathom.

When one can be two at the
same time and when one is
discovered the other disappears,
this is the mystery of the truth.

Our perception is built to
observe only a partial truth,
mathematical equations have
no such limitations, so the
truth holds within equations.

We may know the truth
mathematically, but cannot
perceive it directly, only
a few of us very rarely
experience the truth.

...

Glow of Silent Truths

Equality

We are all equal in the biological sense;
similar biochemical reactions drive
all living beings, yet we are all
unique in our creative potential.

All forms of forced equality are baits
used to deny our natural freedoms.

For ages we have been promised
equality in the afterlife: paradise for
for believers and hell for non-believers.

The quest should be to enable the
expression of creative potential,
rather than imposing contrived
equality in skills, lifestyles,
looks, or attitudes.

Promise of equality of
outcomes is a fool's errand,
and freedom is the only
thing worth cherishing.

...

Glow of Silent Truths

Far and Near

Relative scales of time and
space are often used to determine
what is far and what is near.

Beyond these relative scales lies
an invisible element that renders
all separations irrelevant.

Things that appear far may
turn out to be connected upon
discovering a unifying factor.

The Earth is connected to the
Sun, making them, in essence,
a single entity.

Two people living together may be
separated by light-years emotionally,
while those living far apart may be close.

Far and near is not about
the time and space separating
the two entities.

It depends on whether the
invisible connection
exists or not.

...

Glow of Silent Truths

Implicit Order

Books are full of knowledge,
but it is implicit in the text,
a skill is mastered only
when it is implicit.

All learnings are implicit,
and secrets of nature are
buried beneath the explicit.

Explicit order is the
source of illusions;
the reality subsists in
the implicit order.

All tricks for self-promotion
and selling are mostly explicit,
for their purpose is to draw
attention away from reality.

That which remains
unsaid is the truth.

All meanings are tacit,
for they belong to the
implicit order.

...

The Way

Different religions offer
diverse ways of traveling,
but it is not known if these
various paths lead to the
same destination.

There are many ways paved
by millions of steps, and
there are maiden ways
waiting to be explored.

Pioneers are those who
discover their own ways,
some searches are about
finding new ways, and
some about rediscovering
the long forgotten ones.

Confronting danger is
the way of the brave, and
fleeing from danger is
the way of the clever.

There is no one right way;
being responsive to the
unfolding events often
opens the way ahead.

...

Glow of Silent Truths

Familiarity

Fear eases with familiarity,
and respect for authority
wanes with familiarity.

Familiar ghosts do not scare us
because familiarity tends to
make us fearless, while
grave dangers lurk in
the familiar risks.

For some unknown reason,
we tend to fear the unknown,
while real threats arise from
the familiar sources.

Familiarity breeds contempt for
those who are pretentious, while
it raises respect for a person of
learning and humility.

...

Glow of Silent Truths

Teaching

Great sports commentators
are often ordinary players,
most of the great players are
ordinary commentators, because
those who truly know cannot tell
and those who can know not.

Great coaches are seldom
great players, and great players
rarely make great coaches,
because those who know often
cannot coach well and those
who coach know only a little.

Great teachers are not the ones
who make discoveries, and
those who expand the frontiers
of knowledge are ordinary
teachers because teaching and
knowing is not the same thing.

Real knowledge is self-taught,
as it comes from within and is
hard to transfer to others,
while learnt knowledge is
easy to teach.

...

Glow of Silent Truths

Escape

We want to escape from the present
so we yearn for the past and
long for the future.

We run to forests to escape the
concrete jungles where we live.

We skip school to escape the
drudgery of learning, and
feign illness to escape the
torture of office work.

We binge-watch screens, to
escape the life we lead; we get
drunk to escape the mental
agony of living.

We cherish living, yet have
invented many routes to
escape the life given to us.

Perhaps the tendency to escape
the reality of living is a hidden desire
for that which lies beyond life.

...

Glow of Silent Truths

Learning

All learning is gained
through practice,
we become skillful in
what we do repeatedly.

Repeated actions form habits,
making us skilled in walking,
speaking, swimming,
cycling, and driving.

Some skills need thinking
to generate insights,
practicing to think is the
hardest exertion.

Essentially, learning is a
survival mechanism for
finding the ways around
life's obstacles.

Those who learn the skills
relevant to their time prosper,
and those with outdated
learnings fade away.

...

Belief

Belief is not the same as trust.

We trust the tangible and
believe in the intangible.

It is perfectly fine to believe
in God, it is fine to believe
in rebirth, or in life after death.

It is may be blissful to pray,
donate, serve, or perform
a ritual in accordance
with belief.

It is safe to believe in
hell and heaven, and
it may be reasonable to
spend time and money
for that belief.

It is dangerous to exalt our beliefs
at the expense of others' beliefs.

All our beliefs should be harmless
to ourselves and others.

...

Glow of Silent Truths

Privacy

Privacy is essential to
remain undisturbed
while sleeping, eating,
making love, or caring.

There is a valid need to
protect our reputation,
secrets, wealth, and
vital information.

While we prefer to tell
the world about our triumphs,
we try to conceal our faults
under the guise of privacy.

When we deviate from
our own values, we want
to hide it from everyone.

All that is known about us is of
no value, the world wants to
know only that we want
to keep private.

The world is interested in
breaching our privacy to know
where we lied, made mistakes,
failed, or stumbled.

...
Glow of Silent Truths

Mind

The mind is the source
of all thinking, while
intelligence rationalizes
that thinking.

All impulses for actions are
generated in the mind,
and intelligence guides
the impulses.

Those with strong intelligence
appear wiser because they can
show logic in their thinking.

All dreams, imaginations,
cravings, and intuitions
arise within the mind.

As the mind experiences all
pleasures and pains, it seems
the mind is the real us.

We can rein in our mind
only with our own mind;
no agency outside of the
mind can control it.

...

Glow of Silent Truths

Logic

We live in a constructed
reality of transient truths,
and logic is the reality of
those truths.

All knowledge is progress of the logic,
but as the logic evolves, we discard our
transient truths often unknowingly.

Mostly we are unaware of
the logic behind the truths,
and assume them to be true
as long as we hold them.

A truth is true on the
strength of its logic, and
if the logic is refuted the
truth no longer exists.

Relying on a truth without
considering its intrinsic logic is
just a belief, and not the truth.

As the logic of the reality of
existence is impossible to find,
we remain unsure about it.

...

Glow of Silent Truths

Unhurried life

Often, we are in a hurry
to finish work, even
when there is ample
time available.

We hurry because our
minds are agitated, and
the hurried life drains the
joy from living.

An unhurried mind fosters
better ideas and leads to
improved performance.

A quiet mind makes
long hours of work
less tiring and enables us
to deal with challenges
with composure.

An unhurried life is not about
doing less in more time;
it is about living with
an unhurried mind.

...

Glow of Silent Truths

Traveling

Traveling is a panacea
for boredom and lethargy,
a way to expand
horizons of imagination.

Curiosity of the unknown
fuels the urge to travel
to new places.

While traveling, we get a chance to
breathe the air of different places,
inhale new scents, and taste
foods of many types.

Traveling offers the
joy of adventure, and
satisfies the craving
for newness.

Traveling makes us
spectators of the world,
and gifts us with the joy of
being simply an observer.

...

Technology

Modern technology has
leveled many old hierarchies,
but has created a new
hierarchy of lifestyles.

It has diminished the value of
old skills and crafts, and
questioned the accumulated
wisdom of centuries.

Technology may have
made us weak physically,
but it has raised our
powers exponentially.

Our primitive beliefs and
advanced technologies are
a dangerous mix for the
disaster in waiting.

The relentless rise of technology is
making many of us aimless and
some of us depressed.

Technology has created
the great divide among us,
those who control it and
those who use it.

...
Glow of Silent Truths

Betrayal

Betrayal is a tactic often
used to gain power and
fulfil our deepest desires.

Betrayal happens when
stakes or passions run high,
and we trade our values for
what we covet.

Betrayal often yields
immediate results, as
someone's trust is traded
for personal gains.

We can only be betrayed
by those close to us, those
who know our secrets
and vulnerabilities.

Trust is the most valuable
and hard-earned currency.

It can be betrayed
as long as the betrayal
remains undetected.

...

Paradox of Living

We hold many things in
reverence, yet sometimes
mock them.

We fear numerous
things, yet have the
courage to face
some of them.

We love many things,
yet do not want to be
with some of them.

We may be fed up with
the world, but still want
to live in it.

We may dislike modern
technology, yet we cannot
live without it.

We expect others to be
nice to us, while being
rude to others.

We lead a paradoxical life.

...

Glow of Silent Truths

Mistakes

Making mistakes is a
sign of progress; only those
who are not learning
make no mistakes.

Making a mistake and not
rectifying it is often the reason
we get stuck on a problem.

At times, mistakes give
startling results, making them
doubly difficult to correct;
this is how progress stalls.

We are adept at spotting
others' mistakes and mostly
oblivious to our own.

Repeating the same mistake is a
sign of delusion, while making
new mistakes is a sign of
progress and refinement.

...

Glow of Silent Truths

Power of Money

Money is a unique invention, it makes
us different from all other living beings.

Our lives revolve around
making and spending money.

Money has made possible the
exponential growth of technology.

Without money, there would be
no race to create ever new things.

Money gives us the sense of pride and
security, and raises our social status.

With money, we can bend the rules to
our convenience, buy sensory pleasures,
and take care of our health.

In the race to make ever more money,
we often forget to enjoy all the things
that money buys.

We find money irresistible because
it gives us the power to walk away
from unpleasant situations.

...

Glow of Silent Truths

Sacred is Private

What is private is sacred, and
what is sacred is private,
though sacredness has many
circles of privacy around it.

There is the privacy of personal
space and of the family;
the privacy of friends and of the
community at large;
and the privacy of belief.

Breach of privacy is a sacrilege
and is treated as disrespect
to the sacredness.

This is the reason intimacy
outside of a relationship is
disapproved of in most societies,
for it breaks the sacredness
of privacy.

The self is the innermost circle
and the most sacred of our being;
it is so deeply private that
often it is beyond the reach
of our own mind.

...

Glow of Silent Truths

Self and Ego

Self and ego are two
distinct entities, though
the ego originates from the self.

We care most about our
ego, and its thrills come from
hurting others, arrogance,
deception, showing off,
and aggrandizement.

The self remains largely detached
from the acts of pleasing the ego,
but is delighted by acts of
kindness, caring, nurturing,
and being grateful.

Material progress and
individual successes reflect
the dominance of ego in
our thoughts and actions.

The spiritual quest strives for
the ascendancy of the self
over the ego.

...

Glow of Silent Truths

Liberty

Liberty is not the license to
do whatever we want.

Rather, it is about questioning
all authorities, beliefs, theories,
and practices without any
fear of retribution.

Only a few children develop the
faculties for liberty of thought
because their education is
aligned with the established
political and social order.

As a result, many of our actions
and thoughts seek evidence to
support our views formed
during our upbringing.

While we tend to ignore facts
contrary to our views.

Given the environment of
our learning and upbringing,
it is rare to possess liberty of thought.

...

Glow of Silent Truths

Focus

We observe something only when
we see with focus, thus it is said that
what we see depends on where we look;
looking is seeing with focus.

Focus is the invisible force that has
the power to solve problems,
make discoveries, and decode
nature's encrypted signals.

What we focus on grows;
by focusing on negatives of life
we inadvertently grow them.

By focusing on poverty,
we grow it, and by focusing
on sickness, we attract illness.

By the very act of focusing,
we send out a signal toward the
object or purpose in mind, and
thus catalyzing the desired change.

It seems focus can create a butterfly effect,
where a small effort produces significant,
intended result.

...

Glow of Silent Truths

A City

From the outside, a city is
like a kaleidoscope, having
many shades and shapes.

And there is another city
in the minds of its inhabitants.

The physical and imagined shores of
a city simultaneously foster love
and alienation among its residents.

Cities exist for centuries; people
come and go, building and rebuilding
the cities on the land and in their
mind's space.

A city is full of contradictions:
deprivation and opulence,
opportunities and squalor,
evils and virtues coexist within it.

A city is a place for social
experiments, where many
chase their dreams, while the
dreams of many are the
lives of some.

...

Glow of Silent Truths

The Fear of Freedom

We may aspire to freedom
and may even get it, but
when it comes to choice
we go back to our chains.

For us the meaning of freedom
is to choose our chains, and
it is rarely means breaking
free from those fetters.

We love our old chains,
yet we resent when
new chains are imposed.

We want freedom to
choose new chains,
while merrily carrying
on with the old ones.

We do not want to be free
from our tribe, culture,
beliefs, and conventions
because these bonds define
our identity, so we remain in
fear of losing them.

Perhaps, we do not know what
to do with the freedom.

...
Glow of Silent Truths

Fooled Forever

Despite having faculty of rational thinking, we are fooled by those around us so easily.

Sometimes it appears we enjoy being fooled.

Mostly we acquiesce to being fooled by our beliefs, rulers, media, and sellers.

Those who want to take our money and time find new ways of fooling us; but what is surprising is our willingness, and even eagerness, to be fooled.

Those who often succeed in fooling us talk glibly, pander to our egos, promise great fortunes, and offer assurances of solving our problems, both here and hereafter.

Nature's randomness is beyond our ken so it fools us from the time of our arrival to departure, and during the time in between.

...

Glow of Silent Truths

Culture

Culture is a display badge
of identity, emotionally
connecting us to the rituals
and beliefs of ancestors.

Culture is living with myths
and metaphors, often designed
to separate us from others.

Most of our cultural practices are
imitations, deliberately differentiated
to appear as original, as evident
in the multiplication of languages and
dialects from a common source.

It seldom occurs to us that the
culture makes us performers
in the social theater,
where other performers judge
our performances and single out
the deviants among us.

...

Glow of Silent Truths

Rocks

All rocks come from
the stars, and we are all
made of them.

Rocks are witnesses to the
ebb and flow of creation and
destruction on our planet.

Everything that we use in
life has its source in the rocks;
we have grown from them.

Rocks hold a richness
beyond our imagination;
we collect them as wealth
to enrich our lives.

Rocks are a window to
the past and the future,
if only we care to look.

…

Glow of Silent Truths

Health

Health is one of those
gifts of life we come to
fully recognize only
when we lose it.

Our miraculous bodies,
without us being aware,
deal with most of bodily
afflictions.

When the body
requires extra care for
recovery that we feel
sick and uneasy.

A stream of negative
thoughts and a worrisome
life damage the body's
self-healing power.

Health is a close
companion to an agile
body and a calm mind.

...

Fire

Fire is the only form of
energy that is visible to us;
other energy forms
remain unseen.

The light that we see
comes from fire
burning somewhere.

Fire brings about
transformational change;
what burns in fire
cannot be recovered.

All things that make our
lives possible have endured
fire in creating us.

Fire is the time machine of
the universe; whatever
burns in fire restarts
at time zero.

…

Glow of Silent Truths

Witness

To witness is to observe
happenings around us
without judgement.

A witness is not one whose
senses are dulled by drugs
or whose mind is broken.

Our brain speaks in
many voices all the time;
the cacophony of voices
within define us.

Being a witness means to
listen to this noise and
remain unattached to the
actions prompted by the brain.

The witness lives in the body and
observes all emotions, cognitions,
and actions silently.

Witnessing is sensing emotions and
thoughts without being swamped
by either.

...

Glow of Silent Truths

The River

The river holds a vivid metaphors
for how we may live our lives.

The river flows fast and slow,
runs deep and shallow, widens and narrows,
gets interrupted, and changes course.

Rocks get smoothed, some are reduced
to sand, and others become shiny
and colorful in the river.

The river swells to clean its surroundings,
and to nourish the exhausted lands in its
wake, and merges into the sea,
yet the river remains.

The river transforms wherever it
enters and all that enters the river
gets a new beginning.

The river changes every moment, yet
remains the same; it mirrors the universe,
ever-changing and eternal.

...

Glow of Silent Truths

Pleasures

To experience sensory
or emotional pleasures,
our expectations must be
met or exceeded.

All pleasures are transient,
therefore we always need
more and more of them.

Since pleasures dull with
repeated experiencing,
we chase pleasures in the
novelty of the experiences.

Addiction to any activity,
be it vile or virtuous,
implies we are doing it
for pleasure as the goal.

Easy way for a composed
and happy life is to shift
the primary focus away
from seeking pleasures.

...

Glow of Silent Truths

Night

Night fills our hearts with
a sense of mystery,
in its glow, ordinary
things turn strange.

The night makes us
unrestrained in feeling
our desires, and
sometimes shines a light
on our deepest thoughts.

The night is cooler than the day,
a refuge for agitated minds.

We take a dip into the night
to wake up on a new day;
the stale day's dreariness
breaks in the night.

The night is not just for
sleeping, but for dreaming;
every night gives us a
chance to live a new life.

...

Glow of Silent Truths

Wind

Wind is like a circle,
we do not know where
it begins or ends.

Many things in wind's path
dance to its rhythm,
sometimes slowly, and
at times fast.

Wind gathers clouds
to bring rains and makes
many things soar to the sky.

Wind sweeps away
obstacles in its trail,
creating new vistas and
closing old passages.

We often find the soft wind refreshing,
for it feels like touching the invisible life.

If we are mindful of the wind
and listen to it, long-lost memories
and new insights come alive,
enriching our lives.

...

Glow of Silent Truths

Shadow

We are not alone when
our shadow is with us.

In darkness, we feel lonely
as the shadow leaves us.

A shadow exists only in
the presence of light and
fires our imagination by
showing us only the outline.

Some shadows warn
us of lurking dangers,
and some exist only in
our imaginations.

Unreal shadows exist
in our minds as fears;
lighting up the mind
dispels the shadows of
fear.

Some shadows are illusions, and
some make illusions real.

...

Glow of Silent Truths

Waiting

Waiting is the twin of
expectation; it arrives after
the expectation is born.

We are surprised when
the unexpected happens,
for the unexpected is that
which is never awaited.

All hopes are a form of
waiting, and a positive
mindset never tires of it.

Unfulfilled hopes render
the waiting endless, and
all prayers are to make
the waiting successful.

Waiting patiently is a
form of meditation, and
waiting for a long time
sedates the mind.

We seldom wait for that
which is inevitable, and
puts an end to all waiting.

...

Glow of Silent Truths

Easy Life

Anything that hurts, but does not
kill us makes us resilient.

Many physical and mental traumas
strengthen us in some ways, even
while taking something away.

Currently, many of us lead
a comfortable and easy life
defined by studying for degrees,
office work, shopping, and traveling.

Our easy life of the present is made
possible by the hardships that our
preceding generations endured.

A sign of impending hard times is
when an easy life becomes an
entitlement in the society.

Tough times will make people
hardworking and strong again,
who will carve a future of an easy life.

Thus, the cycle repeats itself.

...

Glow of Silent Truths

Lost and Found

The lost self is found for the
first time when it knows itself
as a separate entity from the others.

We do not become self-conscious
in a flash; the process of finding
ourselves is a long-drawn, halting,
and directionless.

All learnings aid us in rediscovering
the skills that we had lost.

Accumulations of things and
relationships are means to
find ourselves.

Immersing ourselves in
something is an act of losing to
find that which has eluded us.

We can never find that
which we have not lost.

We find only that
which we had lost.

...

Glow of Silent Truths

Metaphor

Beginning with sound signals
for messaging in the wild,
we gradually learnt to record
messages using symbols, and
thus created the first metaphors.

To the uninitiated, metaphors are
like leaves on a tree,
revealing meaning only to those
who care to decipher them.

Languages are metaphors,
stories are metaphors,
myths are metaphors, and
all arts are metaphors of the
underlying reality.

Metaphors enfold many layers of
meanings, and sometimes
metaphors become the meaning.

When metaphors become
truth, the meaning of truth is
lost and we are enslaved
by the metaphors.

...

Glow of Silent Truths

Imagine

The Earth is the only planet we
know where intelligent life exists.

We might imagine the Earth
as one of the universe's giant
computer centers, where all living
beings are its intelligent machines.

We humans use about five percent of
the available brain power.

The remaining brain power, perhaps, is
being used by the universe to run itself.

The universe looks after the
health of its huge computer center,
the Earth, and provides all essential
means for its sustenance.

Rarely, an individual brain uses
its full power for itself, and thus
connects with the whole universe.

At that moment of epiphany,
all separations dissolve.

...

Glow of Silent Truths

Love

Love has many stages and goes
through several ups and downs
in every relationship.

Feeling connected is the beginning,
growing respect is the ripening,
and the willingness to make
sacrifices is the culmination of love.

Our biological needs determine
what we desire at a particular time.

Such cravings often develop into a
connection for a particular
thing -- food, a scent, or a person.

Love is evident when a high
degree of care is directed
towards the object of love
without conscious effort.

Sometimes, love flashes like
an impulse and prompts us
to sacrifice anything for the
sake of that to which we feel
connected at that moment.

...

Glow of Silent Truths

Game Theory

Game theory predicts outcomes of actions taken by two parties in a game setting, with each party having two options: to cooperate or to punish.

In a limited number of game rounds, the party that punishes first has an advantage; however in unlimited rounds, there is no gain in punishing the other party.

The rule for the net positive outcomes in multi-rounds games is simple: punish when the other party does not cooperate, and cooperate when they do.

In a way, game theory appears to validate the law of karma, which plays out through many choices made over several interactions or births.

The law of karma favors those who cooperate and punishes those who do not.

...

Glow of Silent Truths

Enemy

Our enemies are those who
deny our rights and privileges,
snatch our opportunities,
steal our wealth, and humiliate
us for what we are.

The most powerful of our enemies shelter
inside us, if there is no enemy within
the enemy outside cannot harm us.

Some of the internal enemies are:
the inertia of inaction, risk aversion,
lack of imagination, and submitting
to bullies.

All external enemies surround
us when we let internal
enemies control us.

External circumstances are not
our enemies, but are like a frame
within which we sketch our lives.

We lose what we value first to the
internal enemies and then to the
external forces, who just seize
the moment to cause the fatal blow.

...

Glow of Silent Truths

Optimism

Challenges of life cannot take
optimism away from us, because
optimism is the very source of life.

Breathing may be the external
sign of life, but optimism is the
internal sign.

Some of us seek optimism
from the external sources in--
money, power, and success--
while others find it within.

Optimism is high when
our goals are aligned with
our life's purpose.

Strangely, we often know
more about our goals
than our purpose.

Therefore, being optimistic
about the goals we are
chasing is a sign that our goals
and purpose are in alignment.

...

Glow of Silent Truths

Affluence

Having time to spend money is
a sign of affluence; spending
most of the time for earning is
a sign of insufficiency.

There are two ways to achieve
affluence: one is to limit our
desires to match what we have,
and the other is to have more
than we can desire.

Suppressing present needs
to hoard surplus for future
affluence leads neither to
affluence nor to freedom
from desires.

Artists achieve affluence
by limiting their desires
and using their freedom
to create works of art.

Affluence is having skills in action
that give joy and poise of mind,
and having all the time to adore
the spectacle of existence.

…

Glow of Silent Truths

Fullness

We find it easy to give
what we have in fullness;
the Sun is full of energy,
thus, it radiates the light
energy in all directions.

The oceans are full of water
and give rise to clouds;
when clouds are full of
water, they give rain.

Exhibition of envy, hatred,
anger, and deception prove that
we are full of these emotions.

Pretense is a sign of fullness of ego,
and greed, the fullness of hunger.

Some disperse kindness
for they are full of it,
and those with fullness of
wisdom radiate silence.

...

Glow of Silent Truths

Motivation

There is nothing inherently
right or wrong in this world;
the motivation behind an action makes it so.

Many of our actions are directed
by the unconscious; for these actions
we have no known motivation.

Often, the unconscious acts in
self-interest, but occasionally its
actions come at a fatal cost to the self.

The motivation that we feel after
success and winning is induced
by dopamine in the brain.

All we get as a reward for hard
work is a dose of dopamine.

Oddly, it keeps us motivated to
continue the work.

Dopamine is trying to make us fall
in love with what it wants us to do
and keep us motivated.

Who is behind the dopamine?

...

Glow of Silent Truths

Humor

Humor comes when we
see beyond the obvious;
perhaps, inference is its source.

Pranks are common among many
species, but vocal humor seems
to be our unique quality.

We can say what needs to be
said with humor, without
offending too much.

It is a weapon of common
people, used to hold a mirror
up to those in power.

Humor is the best defense
against insults and a sign of
high intelligence.

Humor relieves the burdens of
living and unites us all
as one people.

...

Glow of Silent Truths

Ambiguity

We often think of truth as
something definite, and lies
as a bundle of ambiguities.

Actually, truth is mostly
uncertain and ambiguous;
only falsehoods parade
as certainties.

All truths are about the
many-faceted reality,
in which we live a life
brimming with uncertainties.

For some strange reason
our brains detest ambiguity,
so we find it hard to accept
the ambiguities of the world.

Our mental discomfort
arises from mistakenly
believing in the certainties of
falsehoods as truths.

Embracing the ambiguity of
truth resolves many
dilemmas of existence and
challenges of living.

...
Glow of Silent Truths

Fragile

Anything that vanishes
at the slightest disturbance is
fragile and subtle.

Silence is fragile because
it disappears with the
faintest of sounds.

Darkness is fragile, for
the light of a little lamp
makes it vanish.

Humility is fragile because
a small sliver of arrogance
crushes it.

Fairness, reputation, and
trust are all fragile; a small
taint breaks them apart.

Life is fragile, as it takes
a second to take it away,
and ages for a living
thing to emerge.

...

Glow of Silent Truths

Validation

Many of our actions are
attempts at seeking validation
from others.

Often, we seek advice
from others to validate
our intended actions.

Provoking envy is the
purpose of showing off,
because envy is the truest
form of validation.

Validation also enables
us to blame others for
many failed actions.

Denial of validation
leads to hard feelings,
and a restless mind
yearns for it.

...

Glow of Silent Truths

Meaning

The world before us is
discernible to us within
the limits of meanings
we assign to it.

When trying to find
the meaning of things,
what we already know
limits that meaning.

Nobody is sure what it means
to be wise, successful, or happy,
but everyone has their own tales of
wisdom, success, and happiness.

We are not searching for
the meaning of our lives or actions,
most of the time we try to find
justification for what we do.

Our search for meaning is
mainly to validate our beliefs
and the lies told to us.

...

Glow of Silent Truths

Power

Power is the ability to
impose our will on others.

Three common levers of
power are capacity to
inflict violence, wealth, and
superior knowledge.

Having any of these three in
combination with deception
tends to attract the other two.

Personal charisma and
attractiveness also confer
access to levers of power.

Currently, superior knowledge,
in the form of technology, has
become the dominant lever of
power, making those who
control it the most powerful.

The technology may soon
transform from a lever of
power into an independent
center of power and begin
to impose its will on us.

...

Glow of Silent Truths

Duality

Duality is the essential
nature of existence,
for anything to exist,
it must become a pair.

The one reality becomes
dual to exist, so we exist
in relation to the other.

This fundamental duality of
the one leads to the many,
though it is only dual.

The duality principle
gives rise to yin and
yang, up and down,
pain and pleasure,
true and false.

We define everything
in relation to its obverse;
without the obverse,
the thing is unknowable.

Whatever we search, we must
find that which it is not, and
through this, we find that
which we search.

...

Glow of Silent Truths

Silent Truths

A lie is gross and a truth subtle,
the lie is binary and the truth not so.

A lie is easy to share as it is exciting
to accept, while the hard work of
thinking establishes the truth of a lie.

A truth is like a rock,
unaffected and silent
regardless of what
goes on around it,
a lie is like a fallen leaf
swiftly moving in the air.

When we search for the
truth, several lies emerge
to fool us and live on till
the truth is finally found.

It is quite strange that
the truth needs to be
proved, while lies just
exist without any proof.

Only a few care to defend
the truth, so mostly lies
circulate everywhere.

...

Glow of Silent Truths

Beyond the Obvious

What we comprehend with
our senses exists for us,
but there is always something
beyond the obvious.

Most things obvious to us
serve to facilitate our living;
they do not necessarily represent
what actually is.

Painstaking efforts of the past
have made many things
obvious to us now.

But going beyond the obvious is
an unfinished journey.

Knowing is that which
unwraps the obvious, and
makes obvious that which is
not so obvious.

Everything in this world is
wrapped up in infinite layers,
so we have to keep
unraveling the obvious.

...

Glow of Silent Truths

Failures

There are no failures,
only attempts missing
the target.

When we stop trying,
we give up on something.

Making the same attempt
repeatedly is a wishful thinking;
modifying the next attempt is learning.

There are a gazillion ways
in which a thing will not work;
there is at least one way
in which it works.

Often, many attempts are
needed to get it right,
so life is about ceaseless effort.

Some failures are signals
to change course, and
some to test our resolve.

...

Glow of Silent Truths

Change

Leading change demands
boundless courage, for
change discomforts all
and satisfies only a few.

Often the way out of a
life's predicament is
through a change, but the
change always comes with
several challenges.

Change becomes inevitable
when the troubles of the
present are more frightening
than the challenges of
the change.

With the crumbling of the
extant order, the change
often starts on its own and
consumes most of its agents.

Ironically, those who benefit
from the change are not
the ones who toiled for it.

...

Glow of Silent Truths

Sleep

Sleep is the freedom from
the grind of life, when we
sleep all problems before
us take the back seat.

Sleep takes us beyond
conscious thinking into
the world of dreams, and
sometimes dreams help us
in resolving our dilemmas.

If a thought deprives us of sleep,
then it is a signal of deep worry,
and we must change that
which is not letting us sleep.

In sleep, we no longer
exist in this world,
for sleep is the paradise
we seek all the time.

If sleep is so amazing,
why are we afraid of
the permanent sleep?

…

Cause and Effect

We often hear the question,
"What came first, the chicken or the egg?"
and often get the clever answer,
"A chicken is egg's way of making an egg."

Essentially both the question
and the answer imply that
we do not know what is the cause
and what is the effect, possibly,
effects choose their causes.

What we call a cause of
an outcome is the synchronicity of
two events taking place at the
same time and in the same space.

We now know that at all times,
every point in the universe is
ripe with many possibilities.

An emergent effect prompts
its agents to create the initial
conditions for its arrival, and
we call the agents of the
outcome its causes.

...

Glow of Silent Truths

Wisdom

Wisdom can come from
any direction, for it arises
from existence itself, and
not from any single individual.

Not knowing most
things does not make
one ignorant; knowing
the limits of what one
knows is the wisdom.

One who knows nothing
about the world's ways
may still possess deep wisdom
or a secret of the universe.

Many wise people choose
to remain silent because the
language we understand is
inadequate to express wisdom.

Kindness for all living
and non-living beings is
the wisdom of life, and
silence, the wisdom of
the afterlife.

...

Glow of Silent Truths

Memory

We have vivid memory of
emotional moments because
tears leave a permanent mark,
without the need for memorization.

Memories of pain or joy live
forever within us, for we never
forget what the heart has felt.

A distinct scent summons
long-forgotten memories;
a deeply familiar sound
evokes past events.

Déjà vu is the reappearance of
memory as real events in the
present, suggesting the cyclical
nature of existence in an endless loop.

Everything we have seen
and felt is stored in our memory,
but we have lost the keys to
recall the past, perhaps
for the sake of our sanity.

...

Sameness

Throughout our lifetimes,
most of the trappings of
living remain the same,
yet we see changes everywhere.

We read the same news every
morning, with a different
cast of characters and places,
which we perceive as change.

We are expert at seeing small
changes, so even when nothing has
changed, we sense a difference.

We find changes in the sameness
to feel alive and to keep the
tedium of living at bay.

To avoid sameness with
others around us, we deploy
a range of differentiation tricks
and call them culture.

...

Glow of Silent Truths

Negative

When the presence of one thing
excludes the other, they make
a negative pair of each other.

When light vanishes, only a
cloud of darkness remains,
light and darkness make a
negative pair since they
do not exist together.

Opposites are not the
negatives of each other,
love is not the negative of hate
nor good the negative of bad.

Indifference is the negative of
all emotions, and absence of
judgment is the negative of
all opinions.

The consciousness has no negative,
as its non-existence cannot be perceived.

Does it imply that consciousness is the
ultimate reality?

...

Glow of Silent Truths

Price of Money

Modern life has monetized
ersatz emotions and adventures,
which we buy in the form of
movies, sports, and drugs.

Sometimes, buying with money
erodes the value of things bought.

Money buys us the exhilaration
and artificial pleasures of life,
but we often miss the joys of
real action and winning.

We used to watch sports on the field;
now, we watch them on a screen.

We used to cook our own food;
now, we eat out.

We used to raise our own babies;
now, we hire parenting.

Thus, money often makes many of our joys
and actions vicarious and voyeuristic.

Money often extracts its price from
life's real delights and emotions.

...

Glow of Silent Truths

Complexity

To make sense of universe's complexity,
we mostly rely on simple tricks etched
in our brains.

We are designed in such a way that
we understand easily by means of
non-complex mechanisms.

Our preference for a simple approach
to life reveals that most of our life
skills are ingrained, and we get by
through simplified keys to living.

We cannot conceive the four-dimensional
spacetime in which we apparently exist,
and many unknown dimensions may be
waiting to be discovered by a rare intellect.

It is easier to live in a make-believe
world of simplification than to strain
our nerves trying to comprehend
the unknowable complexity.

...

Boat

A boat is as great an invention as fire,
and it was invented before the wheel.

Boats are faster than horses in
favorable conditions, and
they made fishing easier than
farming and hunting.

Boats shaped the earliest
globalization; ideas and goods
traveled on boats to distant places.

A boat enables us to cross
unknown waters and symbolizes
journey into the unknown afterlife.

Like a boat life can be directionless
or tossed in the tides, in imminent
danger of toppling, or caught in the
swirls going nowhere, or taking us
to new shores.

The purpose of a boat is to remain
afloat as long as possible;
by trying to live like a boat we may
reach new shores.

...

Glow of Silent Truths

Kindness

Many of our actions
cause pain to others,
kindness in our actions
eases the burden of guilt.

Hyenas show no kindness
in hunting, while a tiger kills
swiftly showing mercy in its hunting.

So, it is possible to be kind in all actions.

It is not conceivable to have
love for all, but kindness for
all is not too difficult.

Being kind moderates greed, envy,
anger, and hatred, and also helps
in calming an agitated mind.

Kind people often receive strength
and support from somewhere
when faced with tough times.

Indeed, leading a life full of
kindness is its own reward.

...

Glow of Silent Truths

Mirror

Mirrors are devices that show us
who we are, but they are often
used to fool ourselves.

A mirror makes us all self-conscious.
A baby or a bird seeing herself in a
mirror for the first time is startled.

Our reflection in a mirror makes
us fall in love with ourselves;
perhaps without mirrors,
we might have been less selfish.

Mirror focuses our attention
on the exterior and have
prompted us to worship image
rather than substance.

Imaging devices are mirrors of a
different kind, used by others to
reveal what is wrong with us,
as we are often incapable of
seeing our own faults.

Mirrors are not so much about
self-admiration as they are about
a daily reminder for self-reflection.

...

Glow of Silent Truths

Journey

Journey is not about reaching
the destination; it's about the
progression along the way.

We sometimes start our journey
with one destination in mind,
only to change it as we go.

Upon reaching our destination,
we often find it is merely a milestone,
so the journey continues.

All journeys are of time;
we are just bystanders.

Through some unknown trick,
we experience this journey
as our own.

Time, in its journey, also
leaves a trail of memories
for us to remember.

...

Nothing Matters

We are free to choose our paths
and live a life that keeps us guilt-free.

Randomness determines the
consequences of our free choices,
and we call it destiny.

We are essentially storytellers,
weaving our tales from the
random outcomes that
we observe and experience.

Existence is unconcerned
about our perceptions of
frequent destruction and
unfairness in its manifestations.

Often, growth and relative
calm emerge from the
ruins of destruction.

After many cycles of growth
and destruction, everything
eventually gets annihilated.

Nothing matters in this world.

...

Glow of Silent Truths

Noise

Every bit of information
from the past and the future
hits us every moment.

Incapable of reading it all,
we call it noise.

We can make sense of signals
within a very limited range and
remain mostly unaware of
happenings around us.

Noise is not the enemy of meaning,
but the very ground from which
the meaning arises.

Understanding small bits of noise
expands our knowledge, enriches
our experiences, and leads us to
the unexpected.

Perhaps, noise is the unfiltered
essence of existence, emanating
from the orchestra of the universe.

...

Glow of Silent Truths

Temptations

Temptations arise to test
our resolve for treading
the path laden with
disciplined hard work.

Temptations promise
small rewards instantly,
and are designed to
detract us from pursuing
a hard-to-attain goal.

Sometimes we get drawn
to the call of an unknown
talent hiding behind
the temptation.

We are often tempted by
things that are an echo of
our unfulfilled dreams.

Temptations are not evil,
but a turn to fulfill our
desires, a resting place
on a long journey.

...

Ignorance

Sometimes, it is wise
to remain ignorant
of a few things for the
sake of peace of mind.

There are many inconvenient
truths of life and it is better
to remain unaware of
such realities.

On knowing what is in
the hearts of our friends,
we may lose them;
probing silent feelings
often upsets a relationship.

Trying to know all secrets
makes us cynical,
while the joy of life endures
in the fog of ignorance.

Not knowing everything is
the secret to a happy life;
knowing all is painful.

...

Glow of Silent Truths

Rain

Parched earth yearns
for rain, and life is
renewed with its arrival.

We are fascinated by rain
because it pours down
from the heavens,
appearing as an answer
to our prayers.

Everything on earth seems
to celebrate with rain,
its cyclical return reassures
us of continuity of life.

Rain enables existence
to manifest as life, and
imbues the life with its
natural uncertainties.

...

Glow of Silent Truths

Belonging

Whatever we accept as a
part of our lives belongs to us,
be it a belief, a loss, an idea,
or a relationship.

Belonging is not about owning
something; it is about care
and attention we give to
what we consider ours.

Mostly, belonging is mutual,
when we do not care for society or
the country, we do not belong there.

The degree of care is the measure of
the extent of belonging.

The more we care for something,
the more it belongs to us.

...

Glow of Silent Truths

Diversity

The universe unfolds in
a tapestry of diversity.

Cosmic creativity is the
reason for the immense
diversity around us.

Along with diversity in the
manifestation of reality,
there is diversity in the
perceptions of it.

Because of this,
many things appear diverse,
even though they are not.

Perceiving diversity as divisions is
the cause of many troubles in our lives.

The principle of polarity sustains diversity
and when the poles come together
they merge into the underlying reality.

The sum of all diversity is the truth,
while we seek it in fractions.

...

Sacrifice

Giving something that we own
without expecting anything
in return is a sacrifice.

We can sacrifice only
that which is ours, and
time is the only thing
that we truly have
as our own.

We grow old as we
spend time living, making
money, playing, or
doing nothing.

We get time as a kind of
credit in our account
when we are born, and
we continue to spend it
throughout our lives.

Therefore, living itself is
a sacrifice of the time
granted to us.

...

Glow of Silent Truths

Morality in Art

Art is largely free-spirited;
there is neither good nor bad,
virtuous nor evil, inherent
in a work of art.

Birds and bees and many other
species show great skills in artistic
renditions of making nests,
singing, flying, and running.

If brilliance in art is a
measure of intelligence,
then we seem to have an
edge over others, for our
works of art are diverse
and exceptional.

The cosmic intelligence created
the world as a dazzling work
of art, so judging it with our
moral compass, built for the
social order, is futile.

There is nothing right or
wrong in this world, for it is
merely a work of art that obscures
both truth and falsehood.

...

Glow of Silent Truths

Solitude

Solitude is the joy of being
alone, while loneliness is
the pain of being alone.

Enjoying our own company
defines solitude, and when
we dislike our own company,
we feel abandoned and lonely.

Solitude brings about positive
thoughts, spurs us to be creative,
fosters gratitude, and rejuvenates
us to feel good about us.

Loneliness causes anger and
depressing thoughts, and
drains our energies, leaving
us tired and dejected.

Daydreaming and nostalgia can
sometimes help us transition
from loneliness to solitude.

In the depths of solitude,
inner silence springs forth
for the fortunate.

...

Glow of Silent Truths

Letting Go

To experience the flow of joy,
we must let go of the things
blocking it.

All accumulations eventually become
obstacles to spontaneous living,
letting go of burdens makes
life light and free.

Amassing things, money,
networks, and reputations,
and then letting them go,
is the best way to live.

Whatever we gain and collect is
either taken away or dissipates
on its own, it is wise to let go of
accumulations well in time.

Letting go of prejudices,
grudges, and dislikes makes
life less stressful.

Anything that hurts,
simply let it go.

...

Glow of Silent Truths

About Author

Rajeev Kumar Moudgil, born in India in 1964, has navigated a diverse career path.

A civil engineering graduate, he spent fifteen years with the Government of Madhya Pradesh (India), working in departments of commercial tax, public relations, and rural development in that order.

He later pursued an MBA at Cranfield School of Management, UK, and subsequently spent a decade in the corporate sector.

Married to Ritu for thirty years, he is the father of Divya and Suchitra.

The creation of this book is the culmination of a lifelong dream, driven by his reflective and inquisitive mind and his desire to bridge scientific discoveries with philosophical concepts.

...

www.ingramcontent.com/pod-product-compliance
Lightning Source LLC
LaVergne TN
LVHW041914070526
838199LV00051BA/2606